australians

australians

the people and their stories

Steve and Robyn Holland

SIMON & SCHUSTER
AUSTRALIA

AUSTRALIANS
First published in Australia in 2000 by
Simon & Schuster (Australia) Pty Limited
20 Barcoo Street, East Roseville NSW 2069

A Viacom Company
Sydney New York London Toronto Tokyo Singapore

National Library of Australia
Cataloguing-in-Publication data

Holland, Steve
   Australians: the people and their stories.

   ISBN 0 7318 0820 7.

   1. Australians. 2. Australia - Description and travel
   I. Holland, Robyn.   II. Title.

919.4

Steve and Robyn Holland would like to thank the following
companies for their kind support during the Holland's year-long
trip around Australia:

Visit Steve and Robyn at their website: www.stevehollandphotos.com

Design by Vivien Valk, 1 Bluedog Design
Set in Cantoria MT 10/18pt
Colour separations by Response Graphics, Sydney
Printed in China by Everbest Printing Co.

10 9 8 7 6 5 4 3 2 1

For our children, Kate, Matthew and Meg;
and our friend, Julia.

Contents

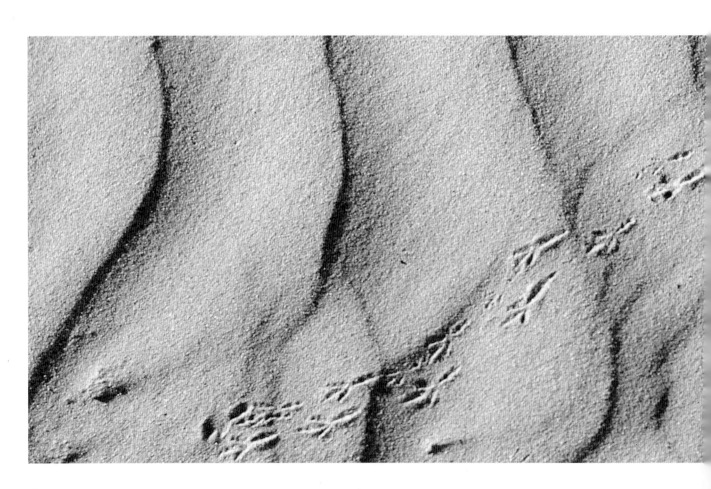

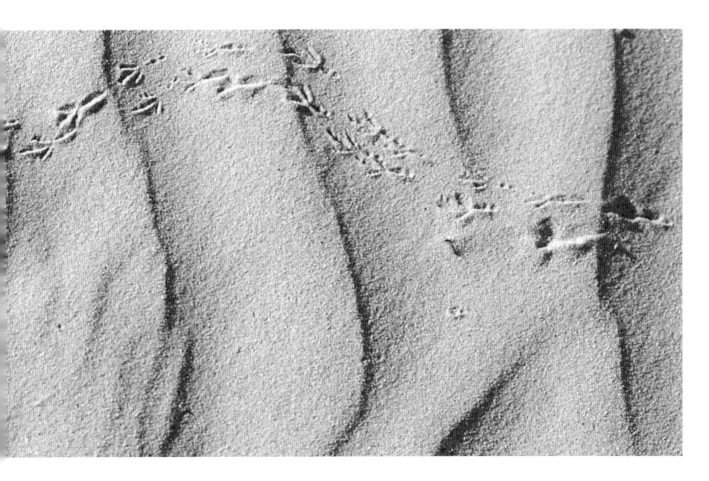

Introduction

If we leave here today
We could be a thousand miles away
Take to the road
See how far it goes
And on this Great Ocean Road
This country's in our bones

So walk with me, talk with me
Tell me your story ...

*(From 'Flesh and Blood', by kind permission of Shane Howard/
Mushroom Music Publishing ©1993)*

In December 1998, we embarked on a journey that most people with a job, a mortgage and young children only dream about. We bought a campervan, sold one of our cars, packed up our home, stored our possessions, rented out the house, found a friend to mind the dog, and set off with our two children — then aged four and two — on a twelve-month trip around Australia.

We called it our magical mystery tour. Our preconceived notions were naught, but our expectations were boundless. Who would we meet? What would we see? What we would learn? Could we find more than just the average tourist attraction, and experience the essence of Australia?

Typical of our generation, Steve and I had both travelled extensively through Europe and America, but we'd never traversed our own country. We could have waited until we retired, like the thousands of other 'grey gypsies' who do the 'round Australia thing' in their caravans each year; but instead we chose to do it in 1999, before our eldest child started school.

Having grown up in Sydney, I had seen plenty of the heavily populated east coast, but not much else of our incredibly vast country. I honestly had no idea

where places like Menindee, Eucla, Mole Ceek or Corfield were, nor what they were like, nor who lived there. A name on a map never means much to me unless I've actually been there, seen the place, and learnt something about it.

Our itinerary was rough. We had a vague idea of what state we would be in each month, but we relished the spontaneity, and never planned too far ahead. A map of Australia was taped to the caravan roof, and at each new place Steve would draw in the route travelled with a thick black texta, numbering each stop. By the end of the year, we had made 75 stops and travelled 55,000 kilometres.

We wanted to come home with more than just pretty photos and holiday memories. We didn't really need to travel to find out that Australia was a beautiful place, a country full of stunning contrasts and amazing geography. What we wanted to discover was its human face. It is our people who give this great island its complex character, their lives that give a unique spirit to our land.

So, we endeavoured to find ordinary people around the country who would share their stories with us.

Our journey began at the Gold Coast, travelling south to Sydney, Melbourne and Tasmania. From Tassie it was back to Victoria and up to the ACT, then to western New South Wales. From Broken Hill we drove to Adelaide, then north through South Australia and the centre to Darwin. We stuck mostly to Highway 1 down the west coast. From the south-west corner of Western Australia it was across the Nullarbor to South Australia, then back to the Gold Coast via country New South Wales before doing the Queensland leg. This final leg took us to Mt Isa, up to the Gulf and across to Cairns, then southward home to the Gold Coast.

At each new town or city we would set about finding an interesting local. We asked them to give us a glimpse into their lives, to tell us about themselves, and show us their territory.

The result is a snapshot of Australia as it enters the new millenium. These personal stories illustrate our history, our industries, our culture and our lifestyle. They touch on Anzac Day, the settlement of the south-west of Western Australia, European migration, the Darwin cyclone, logging protests, the 'stolen generation' of Aboriginals, and the pioneers of outback stations. Then there is just a taste of the wonderful multicultural diversity in this country. Of the thousands we could have met, we happened upon a Yugoslav knifemaker in Darwin; an Indian doctor in Port Augusta; a Chinese martial arts master in Brisbane; and a German coffee maker in Canberra.

They all have something to say, they all have a story to tell. These are the stories and images of the people we met on our journey.

Acknowledgments

I must begin by first acknowledging the little human who travelled silently with us for the entire journey. Four months into our trip, in April, I learned I was pregnant. I was delighted, but also surprised: this baby was one hitch-hiker we certainly hadn't expected to pick up along the way! The baby was due early December, which meant cutting the trip short by a month if I was to get home in time. Steve facetiously commented: 'Well, you're not doing anything else this year, so you may as well grow a baby!'

As it was my third pregnancy I was very relaxed about it all, despite being on the road. I'm fortunate that

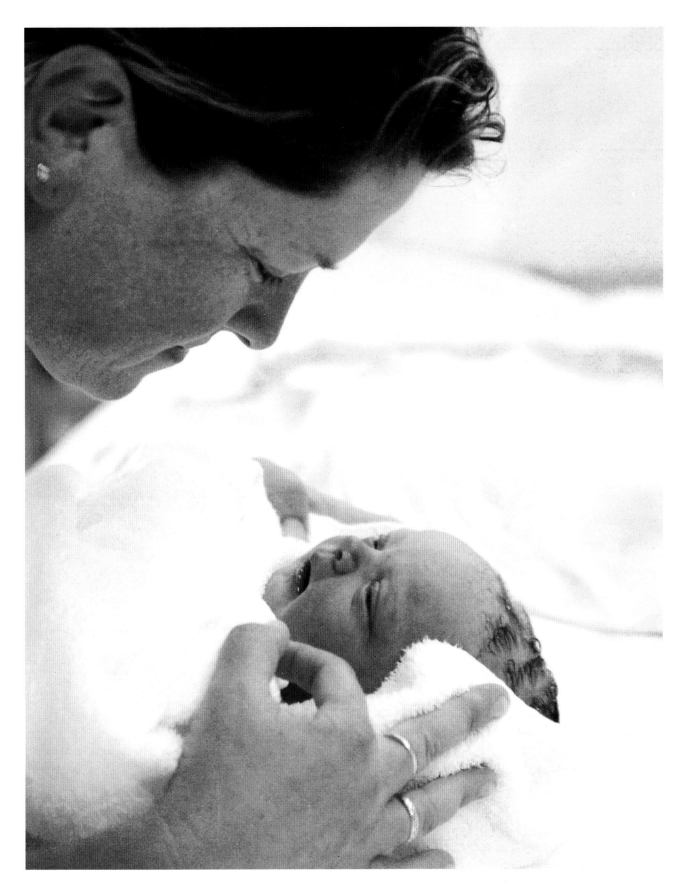

I always feel exceptionally healthy while pregnant. The regular packing and unpacking of the van — which occurred, on average, every five days — only kept me fitter and healthier!

Two-and-a-half weeks after returning home, I gave birth to our daughter, Meg. She was born at 6.56 pm on 8 December, weighing a very robust four kilos. She was a perfect Christmas gift.

Meg's birth was a wonderful culmination to our trip. She had travelled with us all the way, but she never had the privilege of meeting all these Australians. For a fleeting moment, we thought about calling the book 'The People Meg Never Met'. Among my many hopes for Meg is that, one day, she will get to experience Australia in the way Steve, Kate, Matthew and I did — through its people.

This book would not have come together without the generous co-operation of all those people we approached for interviews and photographs. Thanks to every one of you, for your willingness to be part of this project, and for giving us your time. We appreciate your honesty and trust. Although we were strangers, many of you freely invited us (and our children) into your homes or workplaces, and made us feel so welcome. By the end of the day, or sometimes after just a few hours, we had often made new friends.

Thanks also to Pentax, Hanimex/Fuji and Camera Town for your generous support of film and photographic equipment; Healthy Life for keeping us well on the journey; and Golf Caravans (Leisure Concepts, QLD) for your kind support.

To Trish Thompson and Libby Power, thanks for the days of child-minding during the writing process, which was often punctuated by three-hourly breastfeeds!

Thanks to our managing editor, Brigitta Doyle, for her hard work and patience; also to editor Heather Jamieson and designer Vivien Valk.

Finally, thanks to my husband Steve — not only for doing all the driving — but, most importantly, for his steadfast faith in me and in this book.

STOCK AND STATION AGENT

Forbes, New South Wales

Born: Sydney, New South Wales, 1975

'Cracking pen of lambs, buyers. I want $48 for them!' a voice bellows out from the edge of a crowded sheep pen, one of hundreds filled for the weekly livestock sales in Forbes. Sitting astride a gate, somewhat conspicuous in his cream cowboy hat and pink shirt, is Tim Gregory, a livestock sales manager for Elders Ltd. Smooth and self-assured, Tim moves quickly from one pen to the next, auctioning sheep and lambs destined for the abattoirs. 'You don't want to waste time at the sales. To be good at it, you have to run the sales, not the buyers,' he explains. Today's best lamb sold for $42.80 a head, the worst for $29. About five per cent of the lamb and about fifty per cent of the mutton will be exported.

Tim spends two days a week at the saleyards. On Mondays, he auctions cattle; on Tuesdays, lambs and sheep. The remainder of his week is taken up with travelling around the district, meeting regular clients or finding new ones. 'On Wednesdays, Thursdays and Fridays, my car is my office. You always try and get new clients, but it's a word of mouth thing usually.

'Night-times are taken up with phone work. I don't just go home and have a beer. The job is becoming more marketing rather than selling. I try and put forward a marketing program, rather than just selling all the stock in the sales yards. We actually sell more outside the sales yards than in them. We sell large runs of cattle direct to abattoirs. We're also involved in the feedlotting of cattle,

so they go into a registered feedlot and we'll feed them for a specific market, like Coles or Woolworths. This is where your grain-fed beef comes from.

'The days of the sales yards being the place to sell are changing. There'll always be sales yards, but numbers are going more on direct consignment now. Late in 2000, I'll be accompanying a live cattle export consignment to Japan.'

With livestock producers not as heavily reliant on agents these days, Tim works on developing relationships with exporters and large companies and selecting specific markets for livestock, rather than just straight selling through the yards.

Elders Ltd, a publicly listed company with a futures trading group in Sydney, handles rural finance and merchandise, chemical sales, insurance and real estate. It also manages live cattle exports out of South Australia, Victoria and the Northern Territory, and owns the Australian Agricultural Company, one of the biggest beef producers in Australia. Tim has been working for the company since 1997, after spending the first three years of his working life as a jackaroo and stockman.

Tim attended school in Tamworth and Sydney, but the country always appealed to him. He wanted to be a merchant banker or stockbroker; in a sense, he chose the rural side of this instead. He jackarooed on cattle properties in Queensland and New South Wales for the Prudential Pastoral Company, another of the largest beef producers in Australia. He spent fifteen months working on a 155,000-acre sheep and cattle property in Enngonia, west of Bourke.

After completing a stock and station agent licensing course at the University of Western Sydney, Tim was immediately employed by Elders Ltd. He was sent to Theodore, in central Queensland, to do livestock sales, then onto Naracoorte, South Australia, for two years. He took up the Forbes position in 1999,

and hopes to stay put for a while. 'The opportunity to go a bit further up the ladder with the company prompted me to move here,' Tim says. 'I'm one of two agents in this branch and I run three-quarters of the livestock business. I'm selective about where I want to work. I wouldn't want to work on the coast. I like central New South Wales, South Australia and Queensland because there's bigger numbers of stock to work with in these places.'

Tim says he has no desire to work for any other company because the opportunities within Elders Ltd are so diverse. He describes livestock sales as the 'base roots' of the company and, although he is learning a great deal, is eager to move up.

'I don't want to be around sales yards for the rest of my life. I would like to get into more marketing, into a manager-type position. I wouldn't mind running a branch, but I know I have to crawl before I can walk.

'This job has taught me people skills. There's a lot of trust in this job — the client has to learn to trust you. You've got to learn to get on with people, you have to build a rapport with them. You're dealing with people's income, which is their bread and butter. They want to know what price they'll get before the stock leaves their property. There's no equilibrium price across the board.'

Australian stock owners are becoming more aware of the economic need for good management skills, Tim believes. 'If you're going to make money in agriculture these days, you have to be a pretty good manager and operator. We're trying to crack the European beef market at the moment. To keep ourselves in the world market, we've got to be producing a premium product. It all comes back to better management practice by the producers. You only have to look at the Australian wool market — the stockpile is huge — to see how tough it is out there.'

ENTERTAINER/ PROMOTER

Broken Hill, New South Wales

Born: Frankston, Victoria, 1954

Laurie White

Karaoke Night is in full swing at the Broken Hill Musicians' Club. In front of a lively crowd of about 600, a few local girls are delivering a tuneless rendition of a pop song. Despite their obvious lack of talent, they get a loud round of applause. This is one of the big nights in Broken Hill and what matters is that everyone is having fun and having a go. Laurie White, the club's promotions manager and karaoke host, rushes back on stage. 'Thanks darls, that was fabulous, now nick off,' she says in her husky voice. 'Come on everyone, let's party!'

The dance floor fills quickly as an ABBA song comes on. Laurie, her blonde hair a bright beacon above her black sequined outfit, leaps up onto the top of the piano and dances there. Karaoke Night is her success story, and she's proud of it.

'Most things in Broken Hill last for a couple of months, then they die,' Laurie begins. 'We started this in 1993. I ran it my way; I did stuff in between to entertain. Every other karaoke show I'd seen was just people singing and I thought, "How boring!" So I turned it into a floor show. The first night people came out of curiosity, then it snowballed by word of mouth. Now a thousand people come. The 'Today' show did an interview with me a while back and dubbed me the Karaoke Queen. I think the locals' reaction has all been positive. You get your knockers, but they still come every month, religiously.'

Most nights, you'll find Laurie swanning around the Musos' Club, perhaps spinning a prize wheel for the

patrons or running a club raffle. She is the only woman in Australia with a two-up licence, and often runs two-up games in the purpose-built room.

Laurie came to Broken Hill at the age of twenty, when a girfriend asked her to help run the Crown Hotel. She arrived a few weeks before she had to start work, knowing very little about the town and only intending to stay three months. 'I was told there were 400 men to every one woman, which really frightened me off!' she laughs.

'I came without any money and I was too proud to ask for it. I was in this one-bedroom place and I didn't have any food. So, I collected Coke bottles, cashed them in and that bought me my first cooked chicken. Then I thought, "Well, what am I going to do for the rest of the week?" So I ate the chicken, then caught a fly — which took me ages — then put it in the left-over seasoning. I took it back to the shop and said, "I can't eat this because there's a fly in the seasoning." The lady asked where the rest of the chicken was and I said, "Well I ate it, but then I found the fly." So the shop gave me a week's supply to keep quiet. That's what you call survival!

I remember confessing to the owner two years later, and he laughed and said it was brilliant!'

Laurie worked behind the bar for three years, pulling beers for the miners, and soon got to know everything about everyone. 'The barmaids were very well respected because they knew everybody's business. You were like a mother and Dorothy Dix to all of them and they would put a lot of trust in you, and that's how I got accepted. They either liked you or they didn't. I was lucky, I guess.'

Laurie worked at a few other pubs around town over the next five years. As an outsider, she says she felt fortunate to get as many jobs as she did, and soon felt at home. When she grew tired of the bar work, Laurie decided to open a lingerie shop. 'There wasn't a decent one in town, only granny-style places. I made a lot of friends though the shop. I invented these flick-off knickers that you flicked off like an elastic band. They were chiffon with hooks and the man was supposed to flick them off,' she giggles. 'I designed them, but I was stupid because I never patented them. They were a goldmine because people were buying them as a gimmick.'

In 1980 she met her husband, Geelong football player Lindsay White, who was also a pilot and had shearing and mail delivery contracts. Their daughter Crystal was born in 1983. Laurie returned to Melbourne for the birth so she could be close to her own mother.

In 1986 Laurie and Lindsay started a mail run by plane, covering new areas that had previously been serviced by truck. The twice-weekly run included sixty-two properties and covered the western belt, extending as far north as the Queensland border. They also transported the local magistrate to regional courts, and eventually carried tourists. The plane now sits in Laurie's backyard, wingless and rusting. She didn't want to pay the fees for storing it at the airport, so she took the wings off and put it in her yard.

Laurie's first foray into entertainment came when she and Lindsay bought a run-down club, which they named the White House, and converted it into a reception centre. 'Every weekend there was a wedding. It was a great business. We were the dearest but we were always fully booked. I used to greet everyone at the door.' She gave up the White House soon after being offered the job at the Musicians' Club.

The success of the Karaoke Show brought Laurie a number of offers for acting parts in films, television and commercials. She has had small roles in nineteen movies since 1989, all of them shot in and around Broken Hill, a hugely popular location for film-makers since the late 1970s. One of her most recent films was *Hell, Texas and Home*, starring Steve Bisley and Aidan Young.

When Sarah Ferguson (Fergie) visited Broken Hill there were no female bodyguards available. Laurie, the only woman in town with a bodyguard's licence, was asked to stand in. 'Fergie asked me where the dunny was — she told me she'd always wanted to ask that question!'

Laurie believes she has contributed to the lifeblood of Broken Hill, but feels the town has given her much in return. 'What cheeses me off is when people think it's a mining town full of drunks. The town has really improved since they've started to look after the old buildings. It's got character now.

'The social life here is unbelievable. We do things differently. I've taken visitors out to dinner at Silverton on a horse-drawn cart, and taken eskies with chicken and wine, and they say to me, "Laurie, we wouldn't do this in the city." They're fascinated.

'I miss my family, but I feel secure here. I'm very surprised at the way my life has turned out. I've had a few job offers outside Broken Hill, but I'm going to stay put for now. I'm a big fish in a little pool, but if I went to a big city it wouldn't be the same.'

RIDE OPERATORS

Batehaven, New South Wales

Born: Teawamutu, New Zealand, 1953 &
Winton, Queensland, 1958

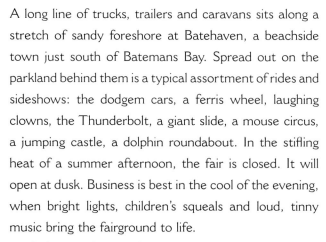

A long line of trucks, trailers and caravans sits along a stretch of sandy foreshore at Batehaven, a beachside town just south of Batemans Bay. Spread out on the parkland behind them is a typical assortment of rides and sideshows: the dodgem cars, a ferris wheel, laughing clowns, the Thunderbolt, a giant slide, a mouse circus, a jumping castle, a dolphin roundabout. In the stifling heat of a summer afternoon, the fair is closed. It will open at dusk. Business is best in the cool of the evening, when bright lights, children's squeals and loud, tinny music bring the fairground to life.

A large white trailer sits several metres behind the Hurricane ride. Two schnauzers are resting in the shade beneath it. Inside, Dave Hodgson and his wife Sharon are having an easy afternoon in the air-conditioned comfort of their mobile home before starting work around 6 pm. The couple operate the Hurricane for Bell's Amusements, which has been running fairs around Australia since 1924.

The Batehaven stop is the longest of the year, lasting seven weeks. Most of the stops on the trail through New South Wales, Queensland, the Northern Territory and Victoria are only for a week, some for just a few days. Like all fair contractors, Dave and Sharon are constantly in transit, visiting fifty-two locations annually.

Dave has worked for Bell's since 1974 and has operated the same ride since 1978, earning the nickname

'Hurricane Dave'. He had been bored with his job as a bank teller in New Zealand and decided to come to Australia in 1972 to look for work. When he arrived, he joined Ashton's Circus as a general hand.

'I thought I'd have a look around Australia for a bit, so I spent eighteen months with them and when I left I ended up in Cooma,' he recalls. 'Then I met Elwin Bell, my boss, at a show there and he was looking for someone with a semi-trailer licence, which I had, so he offered me a job driving for them.

'Conditions were good and the money was better than the circus. They made sure we always had meals, and we earned $40 a week on top of accommodation and food. In them days you could buy a carton of beer for $4 or $5. At Christmas time, we got $10 extra for food, so a mate and I would put $20 in a tin and buy groceries for the week and still have enough left to buy two cartons of beer. That's how cheap things were.'

Dave met Sharon at a show ball in Mitchell, Queensland, later that same year. 'When I was just a young lout,' Dave laughs, winking at Sharon.

It was another four years before Dave persuaded his girlfriend to join him on the show circuit. Sharon was doing office work in her home town of Toowoomba when she opted for the gypsy lifestyle. A year later, they were married. 'I was a little bit hesitant to go on the road with him at first. I was a mum's girl and a homebody,' explains the softly spoken Sharon.

Now, Sharon wouldn't have it any other way. Having been on the road for more than twenty years, she enjoys the weekly moves and looks forward to the next town, all of them now very familiar to her. They have no children, just their two dogs, Chloe and Prince, to care for.

'I don't long to be in one spot for good. I wouldn't live locally again,' she says seriously. 'I went home to Mum's once for four days and couldn't wait to get back to my own environment. This fair here goes for seven weeks and by the time it gets to the end, you're really looking forward to leaving.

'I think it's a good lifestyle — if you don't like your neighbours, the next week you can move next to somebody else! It's relaxed. You meet a lot of people at fairs and just chat to them, you meet people at pubs, you meet good people. You're not stuck in a rut, you're driving around the country meeting people. I've got groups of friends in different towns and I might not see them for three months, but when we do get together it's great.'

The mateship with the other showmen is important to Dave: 'We all go to the clubs and pubs and the girls go to the discos and do all that sort of stuff when we've got a few days off. Some days we do a bit of sightseeing but once you've been going to the same towns for twenty years, there's not much left to see.'

On the road, the couple never travel in the same vehicle — Sharon drives the truck which pulls their trailer and Dave transports the Hurricane. As they arrive in each town, Dave sets up the ride, which takes about two hours, while Sharon spends about an hour setting up the caravan. Sometimes, they pull into a town in the morning, set up the fair to run that night, then pack up the next morning and move on.

'I don't like rainy nights, when you pack up at one in the morning and you have to keep packing up, whatever the weather. The worst time is when the trucks get bogged in mud and we have to dig them out or get dozers in to help,' says Dave.

Dave runs and services the Hurricane and often helps out with maintenance on other equipment. Sharon mainly works the ticket booth but also assists with staff administration. At the bigger fairs, she serves in the food vans. Dave works on a commission, so he will keep his ride running as long as the customers keep coming.

'The cost of fuel always affects our running costs, which makes it hard to make a quid sometimes, especially when you're in remote towns. But we do okay. We're happy and comfortable. We're not wanting for anything.'

LIFETIME RESIDENT OF GLEBE

Sydney, New South Wales

Born: Orange, New South Wales, 1916

Derwent Street, Glebe, is a wide, tree-lined inner-city street, about ten minutes bus ride from the centre of Sydney. One street back from the now cosmopolitan Glebe Point Road, known for its smorgasbord of restaurants and cafes, Derwent Street epitomises inner-city Sydney. Its residents cover every demographic imaginable: students, professionals, newly arrived migrants, young couples with children, gay couples, retired people, single parents, working-class families. The collection of terrace homes is as diverse as the occupants. A row of plain identical terraces on one section of the street is owned by the Department of Housing, provider of subsidised housing. Others have been renovated and modernised, their rents rising steadily during the 1980s and 1990s, along with most of Sydney's real estate.

Merle Strange grew up in Ferry Road, a few blocks away from Derwent Street. She moved into the two-bedroom house in Derwent Street as a newlywed in 1934, and has lived there — give or take a couple of years — ever since.

Merle's parents moved to Sydney from Orange soon after she was born so that her father, a blacksmith, could find work. They lived in a two-bedroom terrace in Ferry Road, which had a kitchen, laundry, and not much else. Merle remembers catching trams to the city from the top of her street. 'Mum and I used to go into the city every Thursday and go to Woolies or Coles, and

Hordern Brothers to shop. 'It was a good area to live in, there were nearly all English or Irish people here.'

As a teenager, Merle regularly attended dances at the Glebe Town Hall. At one of these dances, she met Jack. Jack was fifteen and working at the Glebe Post Office, sorting mail and delivering telegrams on his pushbike. It was Jack who first lived at the Derwent Street house, which his family rented for around fifteen shillings a week. 'We were coming home from a dance one night and Jack said his house number was four, five, six and I said I didn't believe him,' Merle recalls. 'So he took me home to see the number. We were laughing and carrying on, like you do when you're young, and I remember his mother called out from the front room: "Take that girl home Jack, it's too late!" From then on he would call around to my place to see me, usually after delivering telegrams in the area.'

After completing school at the age of sixteen, Merle found work immediately at Grace Brothers department store on Broadway, one of the biggest stores in Sydney at the time. 'I worked five days a week as well as Friday nights and Saturday mornings. I started off in the underwear department. It was hard with some of the bosses, you had to do exactly what you were told or you were out, but Grace Bros was always very good to work for. They looked after me all the time. My first wage was eleven shillings and threepence a week. Nobody served themselves and nobody touched any of the stock unless you showed it to them over the counter. If people were buying gloves, you had to wipe their hands before trying the glove on.'

After courting for three years, Jack and Merle were married in St John's Church, Glebe, in 1934. Jack had been transferred to Bathurst with his postal job and Merle wanted to go with him, so they married before moving away. However, they were soon forced to return to Sydney when Jack's father was killed in an accident at the timber yard where he worked, and his mother needed support. They moved in with her at the Derwent Street house where Jack had grown up.

Merle returned to work at Grace Brothers until the birth of her first child, Maureen, in 1937.

When World War II broke out, Jack was called to serve in the army. He was posted to the Middle East and for the next five years Merle had minimal contact with him. 'We wrote to each other every night but half the time the mail didn't get through,' she recalls. Jack was serving in Singapore early in 1944 when the city fell. He was sent home by ship, along with hundreds of other troops. 'Jack was on the ship for six weeks and he threw a bottle over with a letter in it to me, but of course I never got it. I heard he was coming home but I wasn't sure when, because he hadn't been able to send mail from on board.'

Merle, excited but anxious, went to Melbourne by train to meet Jack, only to receive word that the ship was docking in Adelaide instead. 'I was frightened about seeing him after all that time. I had Maureen with me, she was about five then, this dear little red-headed girl. I'd never been anywhere except on a train to Orange, and the morning we got into Melbourne, I sat on the railway station all day because I knew there was a toilet there and I could get pies and things, so I just sat there all day with Maureen until I caught the train down to Adelaide that same night.' Jack was then transferred to Toowoomba for ten months, so Merle went with him. Their second child, John, was born in December 1944 and Jack was released from the army soon afterwards.

When he came home from the army, Jack's health was constantly poor Merle says. 'He never got hurt, thank God, but he came back sick. He had high blood pressure. He went into hospital and he was in for three months trying to get his blood pressure down. Since 1946, he was in and out of hospital all the time. He also got diabetes later in life.'

With two children in a two-bedroom house, Merle considered moving away from Glebe and finding something larger. 'I looked for places to move to when Jack was away at the war, but my parents wanted me to stay put and close to them. When Jack returned, he got some trucking work with the postal service and I decided to stay put because I thought I'd be on my own a lot. We were going to build a house at Campbelltown, because that was one of the few places that had sewerage on, but Jack wouldn't have been able to get transport into the city from there, so we let it fall through.'

The couple never seriously considered moving away from Glebe again, and settled into a routine family life in Derwent Street with their two school-aged children. Merle was busy and content in her role as home-maker. 'I had one of the first Hills Hoists ever made, I think. I remember the other three or four houses next to us all got them then. I paid it off with two or three shillings a week at Gordon's, as it probably cost eight or nine pounds, which was a lot of money in those days.'

Jack made it a habit to sit on his verandah every afternoon after work with a beer or a cold drink and chat to the passers-by. 'He would sit out on the verandah and talk to everybody,' Merle says. 'Anytime he could sit there, he would. He was a pleasant fellow and whether they were black, white, or brindle, he'd talk to them. He met a lot of people in the neighbourhood but the majority of them are all dead and gone now.' Jack spent even more time on his verandah after he retired as a result of his high blood pressure in 1973. It was during the 1980s and 1990s that he and Merle witnessed significant changes in Derwent Street.

'Glebe changed terribly. There were so many new Australians moving in. It seemed as though we didn't have any friends left when they started to put in the Housing Commission homes. Everyone was looking for cheap housing, and then all the rents and prices of other homes went up tremendously. There used to be a lot of big homes but the government took them over and broke them all up into Housing Commission, which meant there were twice as many people living here.'

But though her community has changed drastically,

Merle still attends the same church she went to as a young woman, and remains close friends with the greengrocer in Glebe Point Road, who bought the shop for thirty pounds in 1934.

In June 1998 Jack died in hospital after falling ill and battling gangrene in his legs. He was eighty-five. Merle is now trying to get a war widow's pension, on the basis that Jack died as the result of a war disability. Legacy is working on her case. 'I get part of a pension but they want me to prove that he got sick from the war. All I know is that he was sick from the time he came out of the army, and never before.'

Merle spends most of her time at home these days. She has a heart condition and osteoarthritis, which restricts her activity.

'I just crochet, or read the paper. I don't go out very much at all. I'm too frightened to go out too much. In the city, you worry about your bag being snatched. I was on the escalator in Woolies and a fellow pushed past me and was running off. It frightens you, you don't go into a shop with ease. I used to go into a shop at nine o'clock at night and think nothing of it. Now you can't go out like that. Even on Glebe Point Road, if there's a shop vacant for a week or two, it gets pulled to pieces in no time.'

In a street that has defined social change, Merle's house seems to have stood still for the past thirty years. The Hills Hoist, still standing firm in the same spot, the outside toilet with the chunky wooden door, the iron balustrade on the front verandah, the paling fence … nothing has changed.

'I'd like to alter it but then I think, what's the good of it? I've got a few dollars so I could alter it, but then no-one visits me much, so why bother?' Merle sighs.

'I'm going to hang on here for as long as I can. I don't want to go into a retirement home.'

Her son John, who lives in Queensland, owns the house now. He has told Merle he'll renovate it one day, but swears he'll never sell it.

ROUSEABOUT

Cowra, New South Wales

Born: Young, New South Wales, 1955

It's morning smoko in the shearing shed at Jerringomar, a 3500-acre sheep property near Cowra. On this crisp autumn morning the corrugated iron shed, undoubtedly like a sauna in the summer, is mercifully cool. As the buzz of the shears ceases, the handful of workers wander towards the back of the shed, make themselves a cuppa, take some food from their eskies and sit down at the worn old table.

With 8000 sheep, Jerringomar is considered a relatively small property. Shearing will take about three weeks, using four shearers, two rouseabouts, a wool classer and a wool presser. Carmel Flannery, a rouseabout, is having a coffee and a toasted sandwich. Most of the workers sitting beside her are family members: her husband Steve is a wool classer; her two sons, Damien and Justin, are shearers; and her daughter-in-law, Naomi, is also a rouseabout.

Carmel grew up on a sheep and wheat property in Goolagong, between Cowra and Forbes. She met Steve at a footballers' dance in 1972, they were married in 1973 and had three children in quick succession — in 1973, 1974 and 1975. Steve, who grew up in Wyangla, had been working for the Grain Board for some years but wanted to try shearing. 'He just had this bug and he wanted to go shearing,' Carmel explains. 'He said to me, "If I don't take it up now, I'll be too old." So he took it up, wondering if he'd get any sheep to shear at all, and he hasn't stopped since. It's been twenty-four years.

I think shearing is in the blood. I was at home being a mother when he went off shearing. I didn't know much about it then. As long as the money was coming in, I didn't care.'

The couple became wool producers themselves in 1978. Soon after the birth of their third child, Gemma, Carmel decided to go rouseabouting. Although a shearer's wage was reasonable, they still needed extra money. Carmel had to take the children along with her to the sheds, which were all within an hour's drive from home. 'I never had to go away for work. There was always plenty of work close by. I just learned how to do it from watching Steve doing our own sheep. I remember Gemma was in a walker and her first words were "drink" because she was so thirsty in the hot sheds. It was very hard. As she got bigger, she was into everything, like drinking drench. She was worse than the boys!'

At the time, the property owners accepted children in the workplace without any fuss. 'You couldn't do this now. I honestly wonder how I did it. Our first three were so close in age, it was like having triplets.' As her two eldest children, Justin and Damien, got older, they would get up to all kinds of mischief in the sheds. 'One January we were working for this doctor, and Justin and Damien came running in saying how all the sheep were in the corner of the pen falling down and that they'd saved them. Well, they were out there riding them, hopping on their backs.' By the time Carmel's fourth child, Heath, was born in 1979, her elder three were at school, leaving her with just one child to take to work. 'We'd take Heath along with us and he'd often go to sleep on the wool bales.'

A rouseabout's routine is predictable, but the pace and physical demand varies from shed to shed. Women rouseabouts tend to be better because they're more particular, according to Steve and Carmel. 'In some sheds, you run all day, especially if the rouseabout has to do the pressing,' says Carmel. 'Your back aches, your feet always ache. Gemma would do rouseabouting in

school holidays and she'd say to me: "I don't know how you do it all day, Mum." '

The rouseabout's work begins with picking up the belly wool and picking the stain (urine marks) out of it. When the shearer is finished, she picks up the whole fleece, throws it on the table, runs back to sweep the boards, then returns to the table to skirt along each side of the fleece and pick out the dags. The fleece is then thrown into a bale and the process begins again. 'You learn all the time,' Carmel remarks. 'Like today. We were taught a new way of skirting. You have to really pick at the edges rather than tear them. They only want a small amount pulled off. Skirting wool isn't bringing in much money, so the less you have of it, the better.'

Carmel's day begins at 7.30 am and finishes at 5.30 pm. It is broken up by a smoko at 9.30 am, lunch at 12.30 pm and another smoko at 3.30 pm. She earns $30.80 per run (about 150 head of sheep), and completes about four runs a day. A shearer earns $163 for every 100 sheep shorn. Most of the sheds Carmel works in are small and relaxed, in contrast to the bigger sheep stations of the outback, where the workers live on site for the shearing season. 'Around here everybody is a friend and you try and find people jobs. I don't think I could handle the way they treat one another in the outback sheds,' Carmel says.

Working in such close quarters with all the family for weeks at a time can have its moments, but Carmel just says with a shrug, 'We get on alright.' Carmel knew Damien would become a shearer but was disappointed about Justin's decision to give up a plumbing apprenticeship and follow suit. 'I could see light at the end of his tunnel but he couldn't,' she sighs. 'Damien would pretend to shear as a little kid. He was making good money from the age of fifteen, which didn't help teach him the value of money. Trouble is, if you make good money, you spend it. If they all thought about shearing, it's good money but a hard way to make it.'

The only thing that's really changed about the technique of shearing, Carmel and her family

Carmel and family

unanimously agree, is the switch from the narrow to wide handpieces. The wider handpieces are now universal, but at the time they were introduced the issue caused a long shearers' strike. 'It went for ten weeks, that strike. We all nearly went broke. During the strike Steve sheared our sheep in the garage to get around it.'

What has changed in the twenty-odd years she's been throwing fleeces, say Carmel, is the state of the industry and the attitude to shearers. 'When I was a kid, the shearers were also the farmers. Not now.

'I think it's really an ungrateful game. Our household hates the phone, because it's always people calling asking you to be in the sheds. Shearers are a dying race. It makes you wonder if you're really going to survive. Unless they make clothing from wool that you can throw in the washing machine, then it won't survive. They've only started to put wool in denim jeans now, but most wool you still have to wash by hand.'

The other Flannery family members are content to stay in the shearing sheds, but Carmel is feeling weary. 'I want to get out of the shearing game, I want to stop at home now. I don't want to be fifty and running up and down those boards.'

NEW PARENTS

Sydney, New South Wales

Born: Sydney, New South Wales, 1969 & Melbourne, Victoria, 1969

Rich Harvey is grinning as he bathes his five-week-old son, Benjamin James, on the kitchen bench. He speaks softly and soothingly, father and child quietly absorbing the new experience of each other's company. His wife Ros watches closely, eager to share in the task but, after an exhausting day dealing with the demands of a newborn, happy for her husband's help. The couple appear to be taking parenthood in their stride.

Benjamin was born two weeks earlier than expected, and just two weeks after Ros left work. Although surprised by his early arrival, Ros believes she and Rich, who married in 1992, were as well prepared as they could be for life with children.

'When we got married we never talked about having kids,' Ros admits. 'It was a "work area" on one of those marriage evaluation studies we did. We were young and

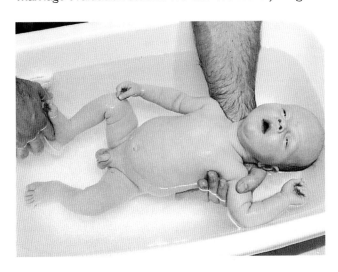

looking forward to a few years of freedom. I've never been a real dreamer about having kids. It took me a bit longer to come round to it, but I never wanted kids to be a reason to boost up a marriage. We really worked on our marriage to make it as fruitful and as rich as we could, and Benjamin has come along as a value-added extra. We didn't go into parenthood lightly, we went into it with our heads screwed on. The other night, we were asking each other, "Do you regret the life we've left?" and we both said, "No, not at all" because Benjamin has enhanced our life, not detracted from it.'

The day Benjamin was born, Ros says she felt a sense of relief, among other things. 'I was a bit overwhelmed. He was born in the afternoon, and that first night in hospital, he was sleeping in the nursery, and I woke up in the night and just wanted to go and have a look at him. So I shuffled up the hall in my jammies and said to the nurses: "I just want to see if this dream is real." I looked at him and thought: "Wow, he's something God and we have created, and this is the first day of the rest of my life." It was awesome. I had this overwhelming sense of love, but also of intrigue and curiosity.'

Raised in the northern suburbs of Sydney, Rich and Ros had similar childhoods. Both were educated at local primary and high schools, and grew up in home environments which they describe as very stable and happy.

For Rich, Benjamin's birth was bittersweet. He was elated but at the same time felt intense sadness that he couldn't share this joy with his mother, who died in 1997. The day after his son's birth, he wrote in his journal: 'Benjamin is a real treasure and a gift from God. I grow more in love with him every hour. What an awesome privilege and responsibility to become a parent.'

Rich does woodwork for a hobby and built some nursery furniture for his new son. 'The night before he came home from hospital, I was placing some of my own childhood books on the bookshelf I had made and found

myself wondering about the kind of childhood Benjamin would have,' he recalls.

Both Ros and Rich were introduced to the church and Christianity from a young age by their parents, and they now share a deep and active Christian faith which is subtly evident in their attitude to almost everything. Rich says he was 'born again' at the age of seven and has retained his spiritual belief ever since, while Ros says her true commitment to God didn't come about until she was at university. 'My whole spiritual awareness changed at uni. Before that I was just a cultural Christian. No-one had ever told me the gospel. At uni this whole new world opened up and it was like I was hearing things for the first time, which made me question where I stood spiritually.'

It was at university that Rich and Ros first met through a Christian group called Student Life. They went out for three months, but Ros broke it off. 'We were different people at the time. I was in social butterfly mode and Rich was a much deeper thinker, but then over the next few years we kind of swapped over in these roles,' she explains. Eighteen months on, they got back together and were engaged two years later. Ros graduated in politics and psychology, Rich in geography and economics. Both chose their vocations with a desire to make a difference in the world.

After graduating, Rich travelled to Eastern Europe for two months with a group of Christian university students, an experience which boosted his confidence, challenged his beliefs and consolidated his faith. He changed jobs four times in the next two years, finally settling into a job as economist with the NSW State Forests, where he remained for five years. 'I've always been interested in nature and natural things. I love bushwalking and getting out in the open, so that's why I enjoyed State Forests,' says Rich. 'I suppose I wanted a job that makes an impact on or has a contribution to the world, and economics is all about allocating resources and using resources fairly and efficiently. I've taken a different road to mainstream economics and

accounting. I like looking at natural resource issues and how we should solve them.'

In 1998, Rich began working at the Environment Protection Authority, which was established in 1993 to broaden government powers over environmental protection. 'My job at the EPA is more broadly focused. It's looking at a whole range of issues, such as air pollution, water quality, or hazardous chemicals, and how we can use economic means to protect the environment. We come up with innovative ways to regulate the environment. I think most people respect the EPA and think it's doing a great job, so I do feel I can make a difference to the Australian environment through my work. It takes a long while to find your niche

and make a contribution and I'm just starting to do that.'

Ros, on the other hand, had clear-cut goals from a young age. 'When I finished school, I wanted to be the prime minister. I was really ambitious,' she says. 'I guess because I had such a stable upbringing, the world was my oyster. I was school captain in both primary and high schools and I really enjoyed leadership. Then at uni, I decided maybe I was more into policy than politics, so I thought maybe I could shape the world by the social policies I created. My faith in God became a much bigger part of my life then, so that factored in to making a difference in the world.'

Ros's first job was parliamentary electorate assistant to Philip Ruddock, the then Shadow Immigration

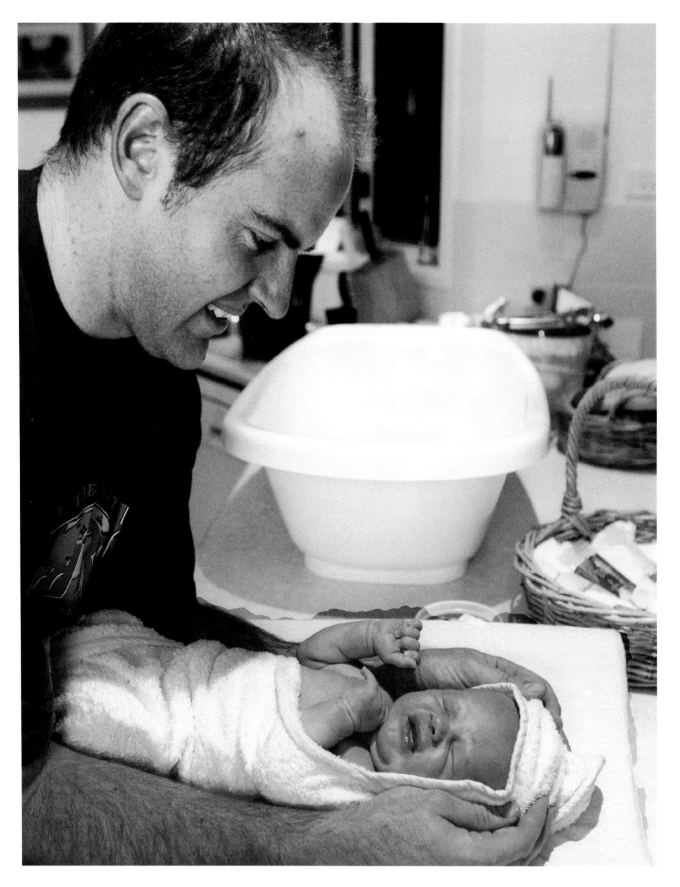

Minister. She spent four-and-a-half years there and found the job a good education in politics. 'I really respected Philip. He wasn't your typical politician, who is being seen to do what's right, but actually doing the wrong thing underneath. He has integrity. I learned about being a person of integrity, even when a situation doesn't lend itself to that.' Her most rewarding lesson came from dealing with people in power. 'I'm not scared by authority or leadership — people in power are human beings as well, and if I want to make a difference in the world I can. I'm not scared by people at the top.'

After doing a public relations course, Ros's career changed tack and she spent four years working at the Hornsby Ku-ring-gai Hospital. As community and fundraising officer, she raised a total of $1.9 million, which allowed the hospital to purchase equipment not provided for by government funding. In 1998, she was appointed Assistant Manager, Public Relations, at The New Children's Hospital at Westmead.

Rich and Ros have high hopes for the person Benjamin will become, but both are reluctant to force their own expectations on him. Rich says for now he just wants to know that Benjamin is getting enough food, enough cuddles and being loved every day. 'I hope he grows into a healthy happy boy, an active teenager and an independent adult. You can worry all you like about your children, but I won't be the sort of parent who says he has to go to uni or has to do this or that.

'My hope is that he will grow up secure in the knowledge that he is loved, worthwhile and a precious child of God. My dream is that he will live a fulfilling life and pursue the dream that God reveals to him, not the worthless ideals the world promises. And my desire is that after I've been a parent, we can also be great buddies and life-long friends.'

'I never want him to feel like he has to live up to something unrealistic,' Ros says thoughtfully. 'Someone said to me they thought Benjamin would have an impact on the world, and I thought that would be lovely for us and great for him, but I don't want to put unrealistic expectations on him. I really just hope he has a happy fulfilled life, that he's independent at the right age, and that he can have functional relationships. I'm a relationships kind of person, so the more we can respond to each other the more our love will grow.'

Postscript

As her year's maternity leave came to an end, Ros agonised over the decision to return to work. Their finances would still be manageable if she chose to remain at home, but she felt torn between her professional career and the new career called mothering. 'I'm happy and content to think I'm making a difference by loving Benjamin at the moment, but is this my calling for life? I figured if I could go back to work a few days a week it would keep me in the loop, but I'd still be giving Benjamin the majority of my time. And I've always believed that if you're going to have children, why put them in daycare full-time?' With the co-operation of her employer, Ros was able to return to work two days a week, while Benjamin attended the daycare centre within the hospital.

WORLD WAR II VETERAN

Dubbo, New South Wales

Born: Dubbo, New South Wales, 1925

Kevin Williams

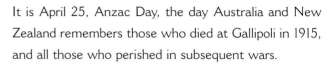

It is April 25, Anzac Day, the day Australia and New Zealand remembers those who died at Gallipoli in 1915, and all those who perished in subsequent wars.

On a cloudless autumn day, Kevin Williams sits in a 1923 model Ford outside the Dubbo RSL Club, waiting quietly for the traditional march to begin through the city streets. Since serving in World War II, he has never missed a march. His health has deteriorated in recent years, so he is no longer able to walk alongside other war veterans.

The march will finish with a memorial service at the cenotaph in the city's gardens. The message today is that war should not be glorified, but instead remembered and acknowledged as a waste of effort and human life. After the service, Kevin will return to the RSL Club for lunch, a beer, a chat and a game of two-up with a few other fellow marchers.

Raised and educated in Dubbo, Kevin left school at the age of fourteen and worked as a telegram delivery boy and a sales clerk at GJ Coles department store, before joining the army in 1944, at the age of eighteen. 'I thought it would be a good life. I had no apprehension about joining. I thought it was a great opportunity for me to see some of the country. Apart from Dubbo and Sydney, I didn't know anywhere else,' he says.

At the time, he didn't have a particularly strong opinion about war, and held no fears about the possibility of being sent to the front line. 'To a point, I thought it was waste of life, but we were needed to do the job, so we just had a job to do,' he reflects.

Later that year, Kevin was one of 1000 Australian soldiers sent to Moratai, an Indonesian island near

Borneo. There were about 2000 US servicemen also on the island. Kevin was an armoured-tank driver and anticipated being sent to Borneo, but the war finished a year later and he never experienced any combat.

He clearly remembers the excitement the day the war ended. 'I was laying on my bed in the tent and all of a sudden, a bullet came through the tent and landed on my bed. The Yanks had gone mad and they were firing off weapons all over the place.'

Kevin had to spend another year in service on Moratai. 'After the war finished, we had all these American tanks and it wasn't worthwhile sending them back because they were outdated, so we were dumping them into the sea. We'd drive them towards the edge of the sea, then jump out at the last minute as they rolled in. One time I got hooked onto a tank with my overalls and almost went into the drink myself!' he laughs.

On his return to Australia and discharge from the army, Kevin settled in Sydney while doing a course in panel beating. Through a social tennis club he met his wife Norma, and they married in 1950. Three years later, after the birth of their first child, they decided to return to Dubbo. Their second child was born in 1954. 'I moved back to Dubbo because I wanted to get away from the rat race in Sydney. I was catching a bus at 6 am to get to work at 8 am, then I'd get home at 6 pm that night. In Dubbo, it took me four minutes to ride my bike to work.'

His family life in Dubbo in the 1960s and 1970s was very stable, Kevin says. Despite the immense change he witnessed in Dubbo, he believes the town is still friendlier than the city. 'We've been pretty lucky for a country town. We've had natural growth rather than relying on government incentives and benefits. There were 8000 people here when I came back in 1953. Now there's nearly 40,000. We were the second house on this land reserve. There were still Aboriginals living in humpies on the reserve when we first built. It cost us 2,600 pounds to build, and 410 pounds for the land.'

Kevin worked for a car repair company until 1969, then spent the remainder of his working life with Ansett Airlines in their engine overhaul workshops. When Ansett moved the workshops to Melbourne in 1983, Kevin was retrenched. At the age of fifty-eight he was unable to find another job, and he was forced into early retirement.

Anzac Day means remembrance for Kevin. He hopes and believes the tradition of remembrance will continue, even though in retrospect he feels more strongly about the futility of war than he did when he was eighteen. 'We don't want it, that's it,' he says.

PRIMARY SCHOOL TEACHER

Menindee, New South Wales

Born: Sydney, New South Wales, 1951

It's lunchtime at Menindee Central School, an outback school whose student population, from kindergarten to year twelve, numbers just 150. Wearing a wide-brimmed straw hat, Thomasina Finlayson is on playground duty. A group of eleven-year-old girls gathers around her excitedly as she approaches, eager to share some personal news.

Mrs Fin, as she is known to students and colleagues, has been a teacher at Menindee since 1973. 'I always wanted to be a teacher. My ambition never changed. When I was in first class, I played schools and I was teacher. I wanted to be a cooking teacher but my brother, who had a fair bit of influence on me, said no-one would ever cook in the future!' she grins widely.

Thomasina grew up in the beachside suburb of Bondi and attended William Balmain Teachers College, which later became Ku-ring-gai College. 'I used to be known as Jane, because Thomasina was a big mouthful,' she smiles, 'but when I started college I reverted to it, because I was starting a new life.'

Her new life began in earnest with her decision to do two years service in Menindee. Her only other option was to work in the outer western Sydney suburb of Green Valley, a brand new area with no facilities. 'I had no idea what country life would be like. I'd only ever been as far as Bathurst. I'd never been outback before and my holidays were always coastal.'

On a hot January day Mrs Fin, then twenty-one,

boarded the train for Menindee. 'I remember asking people on the train if there would be taxis to pick me up, and I wondered why they were looking at me.' As it turned out, she was met at the station by the entire teaching staff.

'There was no teacher housing, so we were accommodated in shabby Water Commission houses. The girl before had left all her food in the fridge and then turned it off, so it was disgusting. It had an outside loo and I'd never had this before! The next day there was

a dust storm. Looking back, it was the second worst dust storm I've ever seen here. If there had been a train out of town that day, I would have got on it. I thought, "I can't live in this hell hole." Everything was covered in dust.' But there was no train, and three days later Mrs Fin began teaching a kindergarten class of thirty-five pupils.

'There was no equipment. We had the old "David, Sue and Wendy" books, there was no library, we had some old plasticine boards, a blackboard, and that was it. You got no help when you started. They just told you to bring your program and that was it. My mum used to make or buy a lot of toys and send them up for the kids, like Barbie dolls. I've got some parents who still own those dolls now, and they won't let their own kids play with them. It wasn't until the Whitlam years that we got a lot of equipment. A lot of stuff would arrive without us having asked for it, and we got grants to develop the library.'

Mrs Fin planned to fulfil her two-year contract, then go and live in Greece for a year. But by her second year she was engaged to Gary Finlayson, a local man who worked for the Water Commission. 'I actually met Gary the second day after I arrived but I don't remember. Euchre used to be the big social activity, so you had to go to the Maidens Hotel on Thursday nights to play it. I met him there and started going out with him.

'We married at the beginning of 1975, in Sydney. Gary's family owned a block of land, which we inherited. We grow citrus and apricots on it now.' With a new husband and a good bond between the teachers, it didn't take long for her negative feelings to subside.

Mrs Fin is the longest-serving staff member at Menindee school. In a small outback town with high temperatures and a sense of isolation, teaching conditions are not easy, so the staff turnover is high. The average length of service is two years for teachers and three years for senior staff. 'You'll get the odd one who'll stay for five years. They used to offer incentives if you stayed longer than two, which worked okay. It's a bone of contention that just when we train a boss the way we want, they leave.' Only once in twenty-seven years has she herself considered leaving. 'At one stage I didn't like the headmaster and I applied for a job to work at the phone exchange, but the postmaster wouldn't accept my application. He said, "I want you to teach my kids."'

Mrs Fin taught kindergarten for twelve years straight. When she decided to change, she moved up with the same class year by year. She now teaches a composite class of grades five and six.

She was unable to have her own children, which is why, she says, she spends ninety per cent of her time at school. While she doesn't feel like a mother substitute to her students, she does get close to them. 'Up until a few years ago I had people coming round to my place on weekends. They used to come over on Saturdays after 1 pm and hang out. I literally know everything about them, but they know everything about me. You know everything before they even come to school. Everybody knows everybody in Menindee. Like my mother — she suffers from Alzheimer's and if she wanders, all the locals will help find her or bring her home. It's like that with everything. We know whose father has come home drunk the night before and got violent or whatever. You're a social worker as well as teacher in many ways.

'Teachers are very needed in a small community. They run on a lot of committees because there's no actual base of people with tertiary education other than schoolteachers. So, if you need someone to write a letter or whatever, it's often the teacher who volunteers. I was secretary of the Progress Association and kept that up for twenty-four years.'

Her long service has earned Mrs Fin the respect of the parents. 'I have had parents say to their kids when they've used inappropriate language, "Don't you ever say that to Mrs Fin." You've only got to say to a kid, "I'll tell your parents about you tomorrow," to set them straight. With country kids,' she says, 'you don't get the same level of defiance because you've got this strong bond and you know each other too well.'

Presently an executive teacher, Mrs Fin plans to be headmistress one day soon. Her husband is preparing to retire but she expects to keep working for some years yet. 'I could never imagine teaching anywhere else. I could imagine living somewhere else, but not teaching. It's so very rewarding — it's like a family community. I can truthfully say that, after twenty-seven years, I still love to come here every morning.'

COMPUTER BANKING SPECIALIST

Sydney, New South Wales

Born: London, England, 1964

In the space of a day, thousands of electronic banking transactions are carried out across the country. As bank information passes from one computer to another, people everywhere complete typical cashless exchanges without giving them another thought. In his North Sydney office, project manager Rob Walford is one of the brains that allows these exchanges to happen.

Rob's employer, First Data Resources Australia (FDRA), handles 400 million electronic transactions in Australia each year. The company is the country's largest independent provider of electronic funds transfer (EFT) and card processing services. Rob is an EFT project manager, who handles the induction of new companies into the EFT system. He explains the role of FDRA quite simply: 'If you put a credit union card into a Westpac ATM, we sit between the two. We're the hub in the wheel. We get the transaction in on one spoke, then send it out on another spoke.'

The value of transactions processed by FDRA in the 1999 calendar year totalled around $A40 billion. The company has 350 clients, which include banks, credit unions, charge card organisations, government utilities, telecommunications providers, and merchant retailers like Coles Myer. FDRA has almost five million cards on its database, drives more than 1000 ATMs and is linked to all major domestic and international ATM networks. When a customer uses a plastic card for a transaction via an ATM, an EFTPOS terminal, over the phone or

via the internet, it is more than likely he or she is using First Data's services.

Rob is a recent convert to Australia who happily gave up gloomy London for a new lifestyle in Sydney. He first worked as a computer programmer for a life assurance company, then spent ten years as an EFT project manager for Nexus when EFT was just beginning its rapid rise into the world.

Rob and his wife came to Australia on a working holiday in 1993, when Rob secured a contract with American Express. 'The idea was to come for a year, enjoy it, and then go home,' says Rob. 'We did that and couldn't stand it when we got back home, so we came back here as quick as we could. You get used to the space and lifestyle out here, and you just can't go back to being confined by the rain or the cold — it's just too miserable. So we put our house on the market, I got a job, and we came back out four months later. We just fell in love with the place.'

Rob worked for the Westpac Bank for a brief period, but was dissatisfied there. 'The environment just wasn't suited to my mindset,' he says diplomatically. 'The thing I enjoy about this industry is that it's quite dynamic and entrepreneurial, and that's not usually a description given to any major bank — with all due respect to them.'

Undaunted by the sheer volume of electronic traffic that passes through FDRA's computers every day, Rob regards his job as challenging, but not stressful. 'I love it. If it's not challenging, it's not worth doing, is it? In a wider sense, it's hard to keep up as the rate of change accelerates. There are things the company does now that I wouldn't have a clue about, whereas a couple of years ago you could say you knew about most things the company does.'

Rob believes companies like FDRA are helping to drive the phenomenal technological advances occurring in banking. 'The things you can do at ATMs will gradually change. There'll be more you can do with them, like paying bills and so on.' As someone who witnesses the passage of information from the inside, Rob scoffs at the conspiracy notion of 'big brother' watching over us. 'The concept doesn't bother me at all. What's the worst they can do — send me some junk mail? Oooh, well I'm scared,' he jokes, then adds: 'Maybe that's a naive view.'

Rob, his wife Jackie and their three sons — seven-year-old twins and a four-year-old — live in Berowra, about an hour north of the city. His trip to work, by train or car, can take a large slice out of his day. 'The hike to work is a price worth paying. We have a boat — which always seemed the impossible dream — and we go out on the Hawkesbury River on the weekends. We have a very relaxed lifestyle. It's a great community to live in and a great lifestyle for the kids. There is no comparison with London. It's fair to say that the standard of living here is lower, but the quality of life is much higher. We have a lot more fun.'

Rob says there is almost nothing he misses about London. 'I used to miss my real ale round a log fire in an olde worlde pub talking soccer with the lads. But there's nothing like a sunny afternoon round the barbie, reviewing the morning's fishing over an esky full of cold beer, with the kids in the pool! We feel guilty for depriving the kids of their grandparents and cousins, but we have a fantastic life, and that is part of the price.'

Rob and Jackie became Australian citizens in 2000. Rob believes in contributing to his community, so he joined the local Apex Club. 'We've built enclosures for wildlife sanctuaries, helped with a rock music festival and put up a flagpole at a school. Any excuse for a bit of exercise and a beer!' he laughs.

With no career plan in place, Rob is perfectly content to live in the present moment. 'I have to admit I don't think of a long-term career. If I'm happy doing what I'm doing, why change it?'

HARNESS RACER

Gunnedah, New South Wales

Born: Gunnedah, New South Wales, 1973

Sally Torrens

The rhythmical thudding of horses hooves is the only sound as Sally Torrens and her father pace around the track for their early morning practice session. The purpose-built track is a stone's throw away from the farmhouse and stables on the 1,500-acre property where Sally grew up. Unless it's a race day, Sally goes through the same morning routine, with her father acting as her training partner and mentor as often as he can.

Sally first got on a horse at the age of five. Growing up, she 'mucked around' with her father's harness racers, and from the day she turned seventeen — the legal age for racing — she was ready to compete. Her father Graham, a farmer who had dabbled in trotting (or harness racing) part-time, tried to talk her out of it.

'All I wanted to do was horses,' she begins, 'so I told my dad: "Just give me twelve months and then we'll see where we end up." Had I failed in the twelve months, he was going to get me out of it, but I still would have stayed in the game. I practically lived on horses. I had ten years of practice before I raced. It was all I wanted to do. I was pretty lucky in that I had some good horses to start out with, plus a good teacher in my dad. Lucky for us we had quality horses too, so we started winning straight away.'

Sally won her first race on her fourth drive. 'I was really confident because the horse I drove, Final Phase, was really nice,' she says, smiling. 'To be able to drive

a horse of that class was pretty good.'

By the time she was twenty-two, she had driven 140 winners. Sally has kept a record book with details of every race she has ever run since 1992. In 1999 her tally was 1119 race drives with 224 wins. She has ten horses, three of them her own, that she trains and races. 'It's been the same pattern for ten years. The horses come and go, but it's been the same for me for the past ten years,' Sally says, in her dry, matter-of-fact tone.

Living in Gunnedah means she has to travel extensively to get to races. The closest venue is Tamworth, which is ninety minutes drive away. Sydney

takes five or six hours and Brisbane is a day's drive. Her parents always travel with her as her support team. 'I couldn't have done it without them. I'm lucky being on the farm because if I was on my own, I'd be paying stable rent and have lots of costs,' she says.

Sally is concerned about the decline in country racing and the apparent favouritism shown towards city racing venues. 'Country racing is going backwards. Tracks are being lost and being downgraded to restricted clubs, which means we're racing for much less money. The TAB was privatised recently and they told us the prize money would pick up statewide. The Harold Park trots (in Sydney) was paying $8500, then they went to $15,000 in one jump. We were racing for $1800 and we only jumped to $2000, so you can see who's the winner there!

'They've forgotten about the country people. Why not help the bush a bit more, because we're the ones who have to travel for a race. Up here, we can only race once a week. If we want to get to a race with better money, we have to travel six or seven hours just to get there. I'd like to be in a position to lobby for better conditions, but I'd rather let someone else do it.'

Sally's father says gamblers' interest in trotting is declining, and bookmakers are on the way out. 'Once upon a time you'd go to a meeting, say at Narrabri, and you'd get eight to ten bookies there. Now you're lucky if you get two. It's reflective of the whole industry,' Graham explains. 'The government stands to take a lot out, but they're not putting enough back in. We really race for the love of it — we're not making much money out of it.'

Sally used to watch her father race, and says the best thing he taught her about racing was how to use her hands, to hold the horse together. She believes it's the horse though, not the driver, that's responsible for winning. Her two best horses were Koara Power, who won thirty-seven races, and Koara Attack, his brother, who won twenty-four, but had to retire early because of a leg injury.

Sally says she has never had a bad racing experience, even as one of the female drivers, who account for only about five per cent of all harness drivers. 'It was hard for a little while — the older drivers used to try and push me around the track, like they were thinking they could bluff me pretty easily. I had to become strong there. Now my best mates in Queensland are women and they're leading training drivers and they've taught me plenty. So now I'm just another driver,' she smiles confidently.

Handling the horses is the most enjoyable aspect of her profession, but it's the winning she finds satisfying.

'There's no better feeling than winning. I don't care if it's in Gunnedah, Tamworth or Sydney, if you can win, that's a rush. You've got to think you can win it. If you go out there thinking you can't win, then you won't win. You've got to give the horse every hope.'

In ten years time Sally says she hopes to see herself with a 'real good horse, travelling around the grand circuit races'. Racing thoroughbreds is another option, but whatever she chooses, she'll still be working with horses.

'Each new one that comes through the gate, there's that little bit of excitement about it because you don't know how it's going to go. You're away from the horses for two days and you can't wait to get back at them. There's something about them that draws you in.'

Badger Bates

ARTIST/
SITES OFFICER

Broken Hill, New South Wales

Born: Wilcannia, New South Wales, 1947

Several kilometres from the mining town of Broken Hill, a circle of twelve sandstone sculptures crowns the peak of Sundown Hill. Carved in 1993 by artists from Georgia, Mexico, Syria, Bathurst Island and Australia, and known collectively as the *Living Desert Sculptures*, they have become a new cultural icon in a town already well recognised for its art.

Badger Bates, Sites Officer with the National Parks and Wildlife, is the only Broken Hill local to have made one of these sculptures. His piece, entitled *Nhatji*, or *Rainbow Serpent*, depicts two rainbow serpents travelling north with a pool of water between them. The hand stencils on the sculpture represent three generations of his family.

Badger belongs to the Paakantji (meaning 'belonging to the river') people of New South Wales, who traditionally lived along the Darling River. He spent his childhood in the bush, much of it travelling with his grandmother, Grannie Moisey, who taught him about bush skills, traditional language, Dreamtime stories and sacred sites.

'We were quite poor and we lived off the bush,' says Badger. 'We would eat goanna, emu and lizard, or fish from the river. My grandmother would put me on the mail truck and take me to different towns when she knew the welfare people were coming. We'd go to Bourke, Ivanhoe, Lake Cargellico. There were six kids in my family and four of them were taken away — they were the stolen generation. I remember when I was

about fourteen or fifteen, they took my younger and only sister away. She saw them coming and crawled under the bed, so they put some lollies down on the floor to get her out, then they grabbed her by the leg and took her away.'

A man who chooses his words carefully, Badger says he is unsure of his own feelings about the stolen generation of Aboriginal children. 'It's happened — I suppose I just have to try and live with it,' he says softly, shrugging his shoulders. 'My brothers and sister had a rough idea of where they came from but it took me twenty and twenty-two years to find two of my brothers. My youngest brother had no memory of who he was or where he was from. There's a lot of bitterness in them because of what happened. I think the government does owe them something, because it never did them any good, it made them bitter.'

Prime Minister John Howard's refusal to publicly apologise for the stolen generation has not helped the hurt. 'If I was in his boots I'd apologise, 'cause it's not going to hurt him to say he's sorry,' Badger says. 'I know there are grudges against black people but we've got our rights too. I'd say, "I'm sorry for what happened, it's not my fault, but I am sorry." White Australia is realising that Aboriginal history is important to Australia, whereas years ago they didn't care.'

Badger attended school 'now and again' while he was growing up. He hated his real name — William — and as there was another William Bates at school, he began calling himself Badger after the *Wind*

In the Willows character, and the name stuck.

Badger was six when his grandmother first taught him how to carve emu eggs and wood. His artistic ability didn't become commercially rewarding until the mid 1980s, when he became well known for his emu egg carvings, then again for his work with wood, metal and stone. He says he is grateful for the support of Gary Corbett, the curator of the Broken Hill Art Gallery, and the encouragement of other Broken Hill artists in the development of his art.

In 1992 another Aboriginal artist, Bill Hudson, inspired Badger to do lino prints, a medium which came very easily to him. 'When Bill saw my first goanna lino print, he started swearing at me and said, "It took me three years to learn that and you've done it in half an hour."' Most of the images Badger uses in his linocuts are animals or symbols of the Paakantji lifestyle, such as rainbow serpents, goannas, fish, animal tracks, or landscapes.

Badger first came to live in Broken Hill in 1983 when he took the job of Sites Officer for National Parks and Wildlife. He cares for Aboriginal heritage sites and European historic sites, and often assists in the assessment of old material. His wife, Sarah Martin, is an archaeologist and is doing a doctorate on Aboriginal sites on the Hay Plain. 'Sometimes I find things in the bush that I also get Sarah to examine,' says Badger. 'I haven't got a piece of paper, but I think we're neck and neck in identifying things.'

Although Badger was initially reluctant to take the job, he has found it personally rewarding. 'I feel I'm contributing to my history by teaching people about my culture,' he explains. He often spends time in the Mutawintji National Park, 150 kilometres from Broken Hill. He says he feels a spiritual link with his ancestors who left stone carvings in this park, and believes the inspiration for his *Living Desert Sculpture*, the first he'd ever done, came from them. 'It was a gift that came naturally to me. But really, it came from my ancestors because they were doing it for thousands of years.

Before I started on the sculpture, the Mexican sculptors said to me, "Don't worry, the stone will talk to you." And it did, it sort of told me what to put on it.'

Unlike most of the other sculptors, Badger chose to make his horizontal. 'If I'd picked a stone standing up, it would have been ruling me. I put my son's hand prints on to show the importance of family. Once a hand print is on something, it shows this place is mine.' Since completing this sculpture, Badger has continued with the challenge of stone carving. He has a carved eagle in the NSW Art Gallery, and a piece at the Broken Hill Gallery.

The wedge-tailed eagle is one of Badger's totems, and there are various images of eagles around his home. His fourteen-year-old son, Bilyara, is named after the bird. 'When Bilyara was born, we talked about

what to teach him, and we wanted him to know both cultures. Even though I don't like Captain Cook or Major Mitchell, he's still got to learn about both sides. I want to teach him to respect people, especially old people. He's pretty lucky in a way, he has both cultures — me being in the National Parks and black and his mum being white and an archaeologist,' Badger smiles.

One of Badger's ongoing concerns is the welfare of young people, especially indigenous youth. The bush, he believes, is the best place for them. In the mid 1980s, Badger took a group of Wilcannia kids on an educational camping trip to Mutawintji in an effort to 'try and keep them out of trouble'. This trip was the subject of a documentary called 'Darling River Kids'.

'I've seen our young generation, black or white, they're just into drugs and all that ... they should be rehabilitated in the bush, not in the cities or towns. They could learn both cultures then, the white and the black, but they can't do that in the towns. The young people are our future and the only way to get them off the drugs is to take them into the bush. A lot of the drug problems just come out of boredom. You know yourself if you're depressed, you'll go and get drunk.'

Having been raised on his traditional land with a deep connection to it, Badger feels strongly about land rights. 'I reckon the government should give some land back to the Aboriginal people because they don't just want it for themselves, they want to share it. We need to learn to live together. That's the important thing now — we need to acknowledge our past to get on with the future.'

SCIENTIFIC SERVICES OFFICER

Parkes, New South Wales

Born: Bronte Park (near Great Lake), Tasmania, 1952

Rick Twardy

As its great steel dish turns ever so slightly and reflects the morning sunlight, Rick Twardy looks up proudly at the radio telescope and says excitedly to the group of visitors: 'Look, it's moving. Can you see it's moving?' His enthusiasm for this instrument of astronomy is refreshing and unashamedly innocent, as if he only began working here yesterday. In fact, Rick has been the ambassador for the CSIRO's radio telescope since 1986, when he was appointed Scientific Services Officer at the Parkes Observatory.

'I get great pleasure from being able to remember something about this place from when I was in grade two of primary school (in Tasmania). My mum read to me from a newspaper that something called a 'parkesradiotelescope' had discovered a thing called a quasar at the edge of universe, and astronomers had no idea what this quasar was. I thought it sounded pretty good. A long time later, I now know intimately what that was all about.' A quasar looks like a star, but has the power of a thousand galaxies, each full of billions of stars.

The Parkes Radio Telescope was built in 1961, twenty kilometres north of Parkes in an area noted for its lack of high winds and radio interference. It collects, magnifies and analyses naturally created radio waves from the stars and beyond. A visitor information centre was established in 1969 to satisfy public interest in the telescope.

Rick's intense interest in astronomy took off when his mother bought him a star wheel to help him identify the stars. 'I was then in fifth grade and I got power over the stars! They stopped being random spots in the sky, like toothpaste flicked on a bathroom mirror, and became predictable. I loved to get a stopwatch and time the appearance of stars. I got great pleasure waking up at night and looking at a star and calculating the time without looking at my watch. It turned me on.' He smiles, then continues: 'In high school I had a reputation for being a person who liked to explain things.'

No wonder, then, that Rick became a high school science and mathematics teacher. At university, he wrote his thesis on a question about quantum theory that had been plaguing him since the first year of high school: what made atoms work? 'One difference with me was that I would ask questions of a different sort and I'm still like that now. I liked questions of curiosity and followed the line of most interest with a class. Even after ten years of teaching, I never recycled notes from a year before, and I was always unpredictable.'

Children need to be encouraged to use science and maths to satisfy their curiosity, not just forced into learning them, according to Rick. 'The way children's natural curiosity dies out is a tragedy,' he says, shaking his head. 'I'm pretty sure it depends on having the constant opportunity to ask questions.'

Rick does his utmost to restore some of this lost curiosity in the people who come to the visitors centre. He loves the day-to-day contact with people and being challenged with new questions or tasks. 'When I first came here, I thought: "What this place needs is a good poster of the Southern Cross." But one didn't exist. It took me five years to find a picture that was worthy. I wrote to a bloke in Japan whose image of it caught my attention in an astronomy magazine. I asked if we could use it and sent him a poster of the telescope as a gift. He wrote back with the slide, saying; "Here you are, I don't want any money." He mentioned he had visited the centre during Halley's Comet days and was

treated well. The poster got done, and it's impressive.

'I also designed a star finder for use across Australia. My one is unique in that it shows the planets as well as stars. I had to calculate the position of the planets every ten days, ranging over six years, and revise some spherical geometry to make it. We sell a lot of those and we're into our fifth edition. The telescope is what gets people curious but it's this centre that satisfies their curiosity,' he says, casting his eyes around the room. 'I'm running a window on the telescope and the telescope is a window on the universe.'

In Rick's words, the Parkes Observatory operates a bit like a 'scientific McDonalds'. Astronomers from around the world come to get the measurements they need, then leave. 'There is no waving the telescope around, just hoping they get something. It's a measuring instrument for very specific experiments, dedicated to the advancement of knowledge and nothing else.'

The Parkes telescope is considered the world's best single-dish radio telescope, and has made a number of significant discoveries. In 1963, it identified the first quasar and, in 1982, the quasar PKS 2000-330, then the most distant object in the known universe. It has detected more pulsars (ultra dense cores of exploded stars) than all the other radio telescopes in the world combined. It has also assisted in a number of space missions, including the *Apollo 11* moon walks in 1969, the Neptune encounter in 1989, and the exploration of Jupiter's moons in 1997.

'The status of Australia being one of the best in the world in radio astronomy still stands, and this is not a parochial statement. The history of radio astronomy in

Australia is that staff in our part of the CSIRO were pioneers and basically taught America how to do it. Nobody tells us how to run our telescope. We don't have to ask NASA what to do with it next!' he laughs.

One of the latest technological advances has made the telescope sensitive to thirteen parts of the sky simultaneously, which will enable a full survey of galaxies up to 500 million light years away to be done in five years instead of sixty-five. 'It will keep a record of where the galaxies are, how strong they area, and how fast they're moving away from us. This has not been done anywhere else in the world as yet, and won't be until they copy our multi-beam receivers,' Rick explains.

Rick's most exciting experience at the observatory has been watching the supernova 1987A, a star that exploded and was visible to the naked eye. His most interesting time was when *Voyager 2* got close to Neptune, and he and his daughter saw the dark spot move across its surface as the planet rotated. 'I have also helped others search for extra-terrestrial intelligence with this telescope. It will be found one day, you know.'

Prompted by Rick's unfaltering enthusiasm for the radiotelescope, there are plans to extend the discovery centre and include a 'Knee-High Science' exhibit for smaller children. 'The reason I've never left this place is that it's too interesting. The whole point of it existing is for something new to be happening and to achieve things. I love this telescope and I like people to go away feeling that they don't have to understand the exact physics of it, but that what happens here is world class, and they should be proud of it.'

ENTOMOLOGIST
Black Mountain, ACT
Born: San Francisco, United States, 1942

PHOTO BY DAVID RENTZ

In a CSIRO laboratory at the foot of Black Mountain, David Rentz is examining some of the several hundred grasshopper specimens he has collected on his latest field trip. David's office, dotted with all kinds of grasshoppers, is a testament to his life's work. One wall, covered with photos of entomologists from around the world, is his tribute to those who, like himself, have chosen to dedicate their life to insects. 'I'm told that from the age of six months I was picking up ants, and ever since I was knee-high I've been interested in insects,' he explains.

As a young boy growing up in San Francisco, David's interest was fostered by the special children's program offered by the Californian Academy of Sciences in Golden Gate Park. 'It had rooms for collections, kids could talk to other students from around the city with similar interests, and it had field trips on Saturdays when you could go out collecting. Whether your interest was botany, geology, entomology or photography, the various departments welcomed people like ourselves to help out, so you got professional exposure at a young age.' David says he is 'still in cahoots' with those who participated in the program, some of whom have gone on to prestigious positions such as curator of the Missouri Botanical Gardens and director of the Smithsonian Conservation and Research Centre in Washington.

After graduating from San Francisco's Berkeley with

a PhD in 1970, David took up a research position at the Academy of Natural Sciences in Philadelphia, which has the largest orthopteroid collection in the world. In 1975, he returned to work at the Californian Academy where he studied Australian katydids (similar in appearance to grasshoppers). Then, in 1977, he heard about a job at the CSIRO's Department of Entomology in Canberra. The job was curator of orthopteroid insects for the Australian national insect collection.

'The way the job came about was the most serendipitous thing you could imagine,' recalls David with a smile. In a letter he received from Australian entomologist, Ken Key, was a slip of paper which read:

'I'm retiring in August and the job is available should you care to apply.'

'This note fell out of the envelope and I showed it to the secretary. She said to me, "You are going to apply aren't you?" I said, "Of course not, what do I know about Australia?" But my secretary kept the note and told me she would apply for me. The next thing I knew, there were forms to be filled out and I had an interview. After the interview Ken said to me, "I'll give you the job, but if you don't like living here, I'll pay your airfare back." I later told him that was one of the safest deals I had ever made!'

David didn't need any deals. Not only did he adjust

very easily to his new country, he also liked what he saw immediately. 'At Sydney Airport a Qantas representative came and looked after me and my luggage. I offered him a tip, and he said to me, "You don't have to do that, you're in Australia now." I had more culture shock moving from San Francisco to Philadelphia than I did coming here. Canberra looked a bit like San Francisco. There were plenty of eucalyptus trees and the topography was the same.'

Australia's wildlife impressed him as well. 'I knew cockatoos and galahs from seeing them in the zoo, but I had no idea, for instance, that parrots were garden birds. I remember walking through the university here and seeing all these birds and saying, "This is my sort of place." '

David has been studying orthopteroid insects, which include grasshoppers, katydids, cockroaches, stick insects and mantids, for more than twenty years. When he began studying katydids, there were eighty named species. He estimates there are now 1,000 species, and he has just completed his third monograph, documenting the distribution, morphology, eggs and different songs of each species. The songs are of special interest, and David has made more than 1,000 recordings of them. 'They rub the underside of their wings against the veins on the other wing, which is what makes the sound. Each one gives a different sound according to the number of teeth on the wings. The structure of the wing is so precise that it conveys a distinctive song. It's just a marvellous, marvellous fauna.'

He was not surprised to discover at least eighteen new species of grasshopper on his latest field trip. 'We know there are 735 species of grasshopper in Australia. More than half of these don't have names yet, just numbers. They're just sitting there waiting for someone to come along and name them. Every time you go out, you find things that haven't been named. Australia is the last frontier for entomology. There are more interesting new things here than there are in the Amazon. Right here on Black Mountain, you can go up and find any number of new species. Every time I get out of the car, there's something to get excited about.'

David is heartened by the public's attitude to science in Australia, but discouraged by official policy. 'The general public is more aware of science than they've ever been, and certainly in Australia we are well aware of our environment. Here, I can be out collecting specimens and people will stop and ask me what I'm doing. In 13,000 kilometres, I didn't get one negative comment, but in America within five minutes you would get idiots blowing their horns and shouting abuse. Australians do have a look, as opposed to the Americans, who would just swat them. I think because of their English heritage Australians appreciate nature.

'The sad part is that everything in Australia seems to be winding down because of this ridiculous philosophy known as economic rationalism. We're losing staff all the time, people are being retrenched as they get older, and then their expertise is lost to the country. Without job prospects, you can't get students to take up the interest. I don't have any young people with an interest in grasshoppers coming in here at all. I'm fifty-seven and the youngest person in this office. I think there should be some new ways to cater to young people with a special interest in science.

'On a world basis, Australians are number one in entomology. We do things better here than any place else, but the way the funding is handled is discouraging. In the CSIRO we have electron microscope facilities, technical artists, graphic illustrators, photographers,

and vehicles dedicated for field work, but these can't be used unless you have the money to pay for them. This economic rationalism was tried in America and shown to be largely a failure. Recent infusions of megadollars into the US National Science Foundation have revived science education and research. This has prompted many institutions to abandon the business of everyone having to pay for "in-house" facilities. It will change here eventually, but by then it may be too late.'

Despite his criticisms, David remains positive in the belief that his research is useful and essential in its application to areas such as agriculture, reproductive biology, and genetics, in helping to determine species patterns.

Work has occupied most of David's life. He says he never felt the need to have children. 'Maybe I'm selfish, but in this game a lot of us are consumed by our interest.' He often returns to the United States to visit family, but says he feels truly Australian now and doesn't miss any aspect of the States. 'In fact the best part of these trips is seeing the red rooftops of Sydney as I fly in because I wouldn't want to be anywhere else.'

SMALL BUSINESS OWNERS

Garran, ACT

Born: Ober-Roden, Germany, 1939
& Prague, Czechoslovakia, 1943

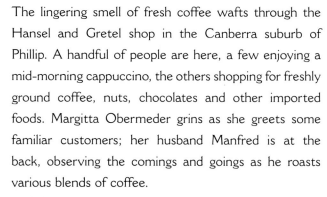

The lingering smell of fresh coffee wafts through the Hansel and Gretel shop in the Canberra suburb of Phillip. A handful of people are here, a few enjoying a mid-morning cappuccino, the others shopping for freshly ground coffee, nuts, chocolates and other imported foods. Margitta Obermeder grins as she greets some familiar customers; her husband Manfred is at the back, observing the comings and goings as he roasts various blends of coffee.

'This bowl roaster is the only one of its kind in Australia. It uses the Sirocco roasting method, like the hot winds of the Sahara,' Manfred explains in his thick German accent. 'You know the taste of coffee always depends on the way it's roasted.' The taste of real roasted coffee was unfamiliar to most people when Manfred and Margitta first came to live in Canberra in the early 1960s.

Margitta, a hairdresser by trade, emigrated with her mother and brother in 1960 and set up a hairdressing salon in Manuka. 'We heard about Australia and about this new city with 50,000 people in it, how wonderful it was for people who were self-employed, and that we would be serving public servants, so we decided to come. We were happy to get away. It meant adventure. I got to Canberra airport — which was a tin shed — and thought it was heavenly. The sky was blue, there wasn't one skyscraper, and it was winter but it felt just like spring.'

Margitta was fourteen when she first met Manfred in Frankfurt. He worked in the grocery store across the street from the salon. When she called in to buy things, he would deliberately short change her in an effort to see her again. Manfred followed Margitta to Australia in 1962. He planned to come for a six-week holiday to see what he thought of the place, but when he learned he could travel for almost nothing as a migrant, he chose that option instead. His flight turned ludicrous when his luggage and the papers which proved he'd had the compulsory injections were sent on ahead of him. 'When we got to Rome, I was taken off the plane and given another injection in the bum,' Manfred says. 'Then in Tehran I got another injection, then again in Karachi, then New Delhi, then finally in Perth. Every stop! When they opened up the plane door, I could smell the air — it was beautiful, but I couldn't sit properly

because my bum was so sore!' Manfred soon found work at David Jones department store, but he didn't really like it there: 'I found them snobby.' Two years later he began work as a trainee at Woolworths in Civic. 'It was a good company to work for, they appreciated what you did and I never felt any discrimination at all.'

Margitta and Manfred were married in 1964. They worked long hours and had little time for socialising. 'We had selected friends at first, but we worked very hard because we wanted to have a house and family,' Margitta explains. The Manuka salon, a success from the start, gave Margitta first-hand knowledge of Canberra society, especially its political life. 'Everybody wanted to come and see these Germans. When they came into the salon they asked us where our horns were!' she laughs. 'We had fabulous customers because we brought the newest fashions and newest ideas in haircuts with us.

'Before the *Canberra Times* had the gossip, I knew it! I got lots of gossip from the politicians' wives. We always put the Labor wives on one side of the salon and Liberal on the other, but they were quite pleasant to each other.' Among Margitta's clients were Tammy Fraser, Sonia McMahon and Margaret Whitlam. 'They were fantastic times. In 1967, I was chosen to do Princess Alexandra's hair when she visited. She was lovely. I was pregnant at the time and she gave me all this good advice about breastfeeding and raising children.' Margitta gave up work after the birth of her daughter, Sabina, that same year. She had a son, Marcus, in 1970, and another daughter, Stefanie, in 1974.

Manfred continued to work at Woolworths throughout these years. By 1974 he was in a managerial role, but was hankering to start his own business. 'After work on Saturday afternoons, a bunch of us always had a beer at the Mawson pub. One day we talked about what we would do if we left Woolworths. I said I wanted to import chocolates. At the time, Lindt chocolate was 55 cents and local brands were 19 cents. They all said to me, "Why should we pay 55 cents?" I said, "Because it's better quality."'

'You couldn't get any nice things here,' Margitta explains, 'only Vegemite, and I didn't like that! So we thought it would be nice to have some good food products. Manfred's workmates told him, "Don't do it; you won't succeed, you'll go broke. Nobody eats that dago stuff."'

Shrugging off the criticism, they opened their first little store, Hansel and Gretel, at the Woden Plaza in August 1974. It sold imported chocolates, biscuits, dried fruits, nuts and fresh ground coffee. They refurbished Margitta's former hair salon and opened it as a second store in Manuka Village later that year. While the other products began to sell, the response to their anticipated bestseller, coffee, was disheartening. 'It took us two years to sell one bag of coffee and we nearly gave up,' Margitta sighs. 'Everyone was drinking tea. We weren't struggling, but we really wanted to introduce fresh

coffee to the market. We knew there were coffee drinkers here, but we wanted to let them know they didn't have to send overseas for it.'

'After two years, a friend said to us, "I have never known a German to give up." So I researched and found recipes including coffee and handed them out in the shop. I made cups and gave them away so people could see how nice it tasted, and what it does to them, and how nice it made them feel! I think we introduced coffee to Canberra.'

The majority of their coffee buyers were Europeans, until the early 1980s when the coffee market rocketted. 'In Canberra, we had higher sales of coffee because our public was more cosmopolitan,' says Manfred. 'Now eighty per cent of our customers are Australians, whereas before it was the other way around.'

As their reputation grew, they became regular suppliers of coffee and chocolates to the Lodge, Parliament House and to a number of foreign embassies in the city. 'When the Queen came to Australia, she drank our coffee. All the prime ministers and their wives have had our coffee,' Margitta says proudly. In 1977, they opened a third shop in Belconnen, and in 1988 they set up a warehouse and office in Phillip. Their success, they believe, has come from a combination of a willingness to work, a love of people and a quality product.

Manfred says he doesn't want to retire, just to 'work less'. He is, he says, still learning new things about coffee, despite all his years of experience. 'In terms of coffee consumption in Australia, we have only just begun. We drink two kilograms per head per year, while in Europe it's about eight or nine kilograms per head.'

Regardless of the daily business demands, Margitta loves dealing with the customers and cherishes her lifestyle. 'When we came here, this place was like heaven on earth, and I still think it is. I wouldn't want to live anywhere else in the world but Canberra. We've had such a good life, it's been hard work but very good. I never want to take it for granted that I am so lucky. Our children have had a life here we could never have imagined.'

GREENKEEPER, PARLIAMENT HOUSE

Capital Hill, ACT

Born: Sheffield, England, 1964

Paul Janssens

It is 7 am on an autumn Monday morning, and the expansive lawns of the new Parliament House are being mown in precise stripes. The new building on Capital Hill, a replacement for the old Parliament House which sits directly below it, opened in 1988. Every year millions of visitors tramp across its ten hectares of turf, most of it visible on the four grass ramps ascending to the massive steel flagpole which has become the symbol of the national capital.

Paul Janssens and his team have just begun work for the day. Paul's job — which occupies him and eight other greenkeepers full-time, year round — is to ensure the lawns are kept in immaculate condition.

Armed with a trade certificate in horticulture, Paul began working at the old Parliament House in 1986. His first duties included general gardening, attending to the indoor plants, and cutting fresh roses or annuals from the garden and delivering them to the politicians each week. 'Just about all of the 130 politicians received flowers. I would get three or four flowers, knock on their doors and hand them to the staff. The best person I used to deliver to was Senator Flo Bjelke-Petersen. She was like your grandmother, and always talked to you. I thought it was the best job you could have, giving out flowers for free. In the new House, the flowers are bought and we only supply them to the Prime Minister's office, the Speaker of the House of Representatives, their deputies, and the President of the Senate.'

After a year at the old House, Paul moved into the new House as a leading hand. The gardening team spent twelve months planting the new gardens before opening day. In keeping with the building's aim to blend naturally with the environment, the design brief for the garden was to return the peripheral areas to 'native landscape' and to make the courtyards 'simple, uniform and functional'.

'When we first came to the new House, everything was stark and barren and exposed. The plants were only a foot high and a lot of people didn't like the landscape, but the point is that we had moved from a sixty-year-old garden to a brand new one. I think now this landscape is as good as the last one, even though it's very different,' Paul explains.

Paul spent eight years working in the horticulture side. In 1995, four years after getting his trade certificate in greenkeeping, he won a position as turf supervisor.

Eager to further his career, Paul completed a horticulture diploma in 1998. 'I want to keep my knowledge up-to-date, especially in the area of turf because there's a lot more money being put into turf research now. I've got more control over decisions now, which means I can use my training a lot more. A lot of what I determine actually gets put into place.

'Sometimes it can be pressured being a supervisor. Over summer it can be extremely stressful, like I'll watch the weather on the news and hear it's going to be thirty-five degrees the next day and wonder if the irrigation system will keep working. If big sections of lawn die off here, I'm the one who'll cop it. The House is very exposed — you can see it from most roads around here — so we have to keep it looking good all the time.'

The characteristic stripes on the turf encourage serious in-house rivalry among the greenkeepers. 'On

the mower, there are rollers which lay the grass on an angle and make the stripes. The first couple of guys who started doing the lines ten years ago were pretty particular about it, so ever since then there's been some competition about it. If your lines turn out crooked, you get stirred by your workmates,' Paul smiles.

In spring and summer, the grass is mowed three times a week; in winter, once a week. A weather station on the roof measures the temperature, sunlight and evaporation levels, which then provides data to a computer which controls the sprinklers. Over the past five years, explains Paul, all the turf has been gradually replaced. 'We used to spend about $20,000 a year deterring the Argentine stem weevil, which wiped out a lot of grass, but through biological means we've found a more resistant species of grass. The new grass has a natural fungus in it which deters insects from eating it.'

Paul is encouraged by the feedback from the politicians and administration staff on the state of the gardens. The landscape services area is regarded as one of the most professional areas within the department. 'We get some criticism too, which I don't mind because it gives you something to work towards and it means people are keeping an eye on you.'

In an effort to attract a better standard of worker, Paul's department broke away from the Australian Worker's Union (AWU) award wage and negotiated its own award in 1992. 'We called it the parliamentary gardener's award and we argued to have our wage structure higher than the industry so we could attract a better quality person here. Because the place is so prestigious we wanted the best.'

Working in Canberra, especially at its political hub, makes it hard to get away from politics, Paul admits. 'It always gives you a bit of a buzz to see people like John Howard or Paul Keating around the place. But if we all talked about politics every day, we'd get on each others nerves and bore ourselves. Actually, if I had my time over again, politics is what I'd get into. I mean, there's a lot of rorts that go on and it would probably be for that reason I'd get into it. I wouldn't mind spending three years here, then getting free air travel for the rest of your life! And the superannuation benefits are excellent, but then again you have to get a whole electorate to vote for you, so there's a bit of a trick to that.'

There is an unfortunate stigma, Paul feels, attached to living and working in Canberra. 'Whenever we go on holidays, I don't usually tell people where I'm from, which is sad I reckon, because Canberra has this image of being spoiled. It's really a lack of understanding about the place.

'Since we changed to local government in 1993, it's all changed. Before that, the roads were federally funded and there was plenty of money around. Growing up here as a kid, every garden was green and well watered but now you have to pay extra for water, and the roads have deteriorated. We don't have it as good here now as what people might think.'

While Paul's wife Lindy would like to move away from Canberra and its cold winters for a while, Paul says he is content to stay because he believes it's a great place to raise his two young sons. However if the right kind of job came along — preferably one as a greenkeeper at a golf course — he would be willing to move cities.

UPHOLSTERER

Melbourne, Victoria

Born: Kalamata, Greece, 1942

A grapevine and a pear tree, both heavily laden with fruit, welcome you into Dimitrious — 'Jim' — Antonopoulos's private backyard in the Melbourne suburb of Oakleigh. Beneath this greenery is a barrel of homemade wine and beyond it, at the back fence, a dozen beehives are stacked next to a greenhouse full of thriving vegetables. Jim sits in the centre, at a table beneath a wildberry tree, drinking Greek coffee with his wife Athanasia (Sia). It is relaxed and peaceful in their small sanctuary, and they could almost be in a courtyard, or taverna, in a quiet Greek village.

Not that Jim wants to be back in the country of his birth, which he left in 1965 as one of thousands of Europeans who migrated to Sydney and Melbourne in the 1950s and early 1960s.

'My brother had already arrived here in 1956, then my sister and another brother came out after him. My mother came in 1963, a year after my father died. They all told me it was good place, that there were lots of opportunities here. The government was encouraging us to go to Australia at the time. So I came straight to Melbourne after finishing my three years compulsory service in the army.'

Jim grew up in the town of Kalamata. One of six children, his childhood was difficult and, in the early days, very traumatic. He has vivid memories of many people in his village being robbed and killed. At the age of thirty, Jim's father, a farmer, was blinded after being assaulted

by guerillas in the Greek civil war after World War II.

'I can't say my childhood was happy but we all loved each other and we were very close, which made it okay,' Jim sighs. With his father unable to bring in an income, Jim had to leave school at the age of twelve and find work. He found it in a blacksmith's shop, building fences and machinery.

At eighteen, he went to Germany and worked as a builder before returning to Greece to do his compulsory army duty. With four family members already in Australia by the time he was released, the decision to emigrate was relatively easy.

Jim's passage on the ship *Ellinis* took twenty-seven days. On board he befriended a man, Con Spiropolous. Jim was Con's best man at his wedding two years later. They now live in the same suburb and are still best friends today.

'I remember, on the ship, feeling happy because I was single, without any responsibility, but I was worried for people with kids. I didn't worry about myself because I knew I could stay with my brother. It was much harder for him when he came [ten years earlier], because he was one of the first to arrive and he didn't understand English. I found it scary to go to the corner store and ask for milk and bread because I had no English. After three days here, I went to buy a beer and somehow ended up with a milkshake in a steel cup!' he chuckles.

Jim's brother, Louie, managed a milk bar and also established a Greek club in Prahran, where Jim worked behind the bar. Here, he befriended other new migrants. 'There was no trust between the Australians and us at first. But after some years, that trust grew and we felt welcome. I was thankful when people would try to help me in shops when I was buying things.'

Like many new Australians, Jim landed a job at the General Motors automotive factory. He spent six months there before going bush to Colac, south-west of Melbourne, where he logged trees for power poles. 'It was very hard and dangerous work. Six months was enough there, so I came back to work at GM again.'

A year before emigrating, Jim had met Sia on a bus in Athens. They got chatting, exchanged phone numbers and Jim convinced Sia to come to Australia soon after he arrived. They were married in a traditional Orthodox ceremony in 1967. Two months after the wedding, Jim went to Hamersley in Western Australia to work at a steel plant, while Sia remained in Melbourne. Four months later, he returned home and began attending a technical college where he got a certificate in plumbing.

After working for a plumber for the next seven years, Jim switched jobs yet again and, in 1974, found work with an upholsterer. Although he never gained any formal qualifications in the upholstery trade, Jim has managed to make a very decent living from it for more than twenty years.

Jim and Sia have three children: George, Chris and Melanie. Their son George, born in 1968, has cerebral palsy and is severely intellectually disabled. Sia cared for him at home until he was eight years old, but the burden became too great. He has lived in a home since then, but Jim and Sia have maintained a very close relationship with him.

Both adult daughters, Chris and Mel, still live at home out of choice. Keeping his family united is of utmost importance to Jim. 'Once you're a family, you're one, and you shouldn't go off and do your own thing. Everyone is too selfish these days. Everybody earns money for themselves and they have none left to share with each other. No-one has feelings for each other anymore.'

Since the late 1970s, Jim has worked independently from home, in the garage next to his little self-sufficient garden sanctuary. Lying across the rafters, above his solid workbench, are assorted rolls of upholstery fabric. He uses a pair of scissors that were made in the 1930s,

and a Singer sewing machine that he can't date, but is undoubtedly antique.

Now financially secure with investments in some local properties, Jim is scaling down his upholstery business these days. He relies on word of mouth to bring in a trickle of trade. 'Money and work used to be the number one thing for me, but now the children are grown and working, I'm taking it easier. Everybody should work but I think I worked too much. I would like to travel more now.'

Jim returned to Greece in 1982 and felt disillusioned with what he saw. 'I went back to Greece and nobody knew me. I've been here so long now that I do feel Australian, but often another side of me feels I don't really have a country.

'But I wouldn't live anywhere else. I love Melbourne, except for the cold weather. Sia has arthritis, so it's hard for her. Melbourne is a big place, a green place, with good people and good air.'

WINEMAKER
Taminick Valley, Victoria
Born: Wangaratta, Victoria, 1919

In the dry heat of a midsummer Sunday afternoon, wine-tasters and potential buyers eagerly enter the large, cool storage cellar of the Taminick Valley winery in Victoria's high country.

Inside, sitting by the door, winemaker Cliff Booth greets each visitor warmly, always with a smile, usually with a friendly joke. The shaft of sunlight shining through the doorway illuminates his thick white hair, but his eyes have a glow all their own. A string of customers walk in and Cliff makes a point of speaking to each one. To him, they're never customers, they're always real people, and he treats them accordingly.

'There are people who've been with us for twenty or thirty years and are still coming back,' he says. 'We don't really treat them as our bread and butter, we treat them more as our friends.'

Cliff made his first batch of wine at age fifteen, having been raised on the Taminick Valley vineyard his father Esca bought in 1903. Esca and his wife Adelaide had previously been managing the Grodno vineyard in Liverpool, west of Sydney, and often visited the Taminick Valley on wine buying trips. 'My father was very taken with the wines from the area and knew this place was for him,' says Cliff.

The seventh of nine children, Cliff says there were always plenty of hands to help out on what was then a 3,000-acre property; nowadays it is about 250 acres. 'We always seemed to have some little chore to do,

and picking from grapevines was certainly much more pleasant than milking cows.'

With only the two eldest in the family getting a secondary education, Cliff left school at age fourteen and began working full-time with his father. 'My first batch of wine must have turned out alright, because the old fella said to me: "If you can do that, then I don't need to be in here anymore, I could be out working with the men."'

'During the Depression, eighteen fellows would come up from Melbourne on the back of a transport and we'd pick them up and they'd live here for the harvest. My mum and aunty used to cook for them and I had to do the slaughter. I'd kill two lambs every night for all of them. In those days, we sold the wine in bulk quantities, in sixty- and seventy-gallon hogs heads, to the wine merchants. We would load them onto trucks which took them to the railway station at Glenrowan.'

After spending three and a half years in the army, twenty-four-year-old Cliff returned to the vineyard to work alongside his father. Although he was the only one of his siblings to stay in the wine business, he never considered an alternative career. 'I think in that day and age, you just did something and whether you felt it was your calling or not, you accepted it and got on with the job. I think it was the same for all of us at that time. There were no finances to send us to university or such.' He married Jean in 1942 and they had six children, four girls and two boys.

Cliff first began bottling the wine under the family name in 1968. Promotion has never been high on Cliff's list of priorities — he relies more on word of mouth than on advertising. Sales are made only by mail order or at the cellar door, but Taminick wines have sold consistently well for more than thirty years. In 1997 the Shiraz won the best Victorian red in the Great Australian Shiraz Challenge. Despite his achievements, Cliff says he's still learning.

'Winemaking is one of those things where you learn the fundamentals early — the dos and the don'ts — but

you never really finish learning. There's things going on that I'm still picking up. It's not an easy occupation. We still make the wines using open fermentation, where the cap is plunged, and that happens about four times a day. It's very labour intensive. Not many winemakers use this style — you count them on your hand now. These days, most wines are made in stainless-steel fermenters, which make good wines but you rarely get a classic this way. I call it a lazy man's way of making wine.'

The only way to make a good wine, he says, is to start with a good-quality fruit. 'It's like the old saying, never make a silk purse from a sow's ear. Our fruit is always good because we can control the moisture.

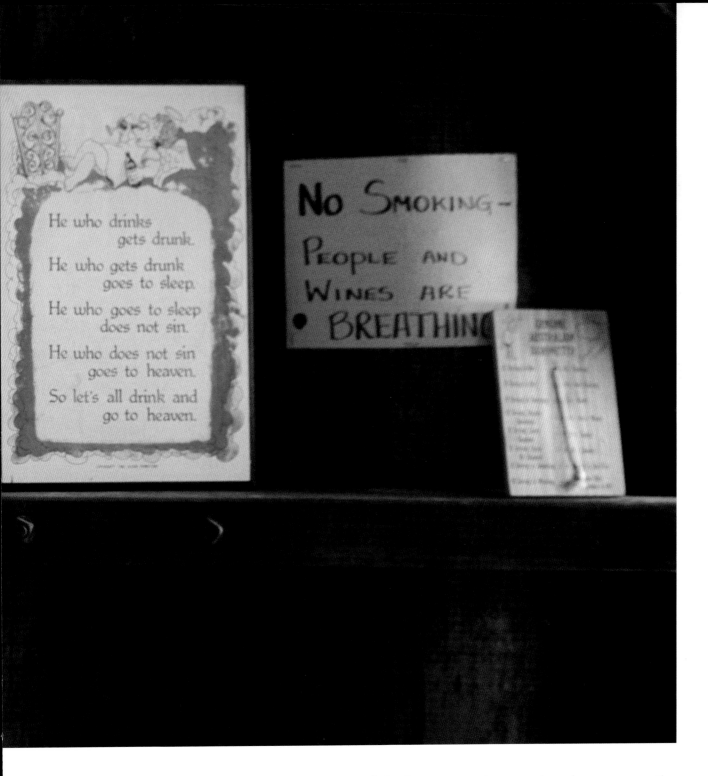

We pump the water up from Lake Mokoan, so even during a drought, we have supplementary watering. We don't go for big tonnages ... we get two and a half to three tonnes per acre, which isn't really much.'

Cliff is critical of the lack of government support for the Australian wine industry. 'For a long time we have known that Australian wines are world class, but our federal government has never been keen on promoting them, so the industry has done its own promotion. Our wines, especially the reds, are world renowned and they've given the European ones a bit of a hiding.

'Although we only have a small proportion of the world's trade, it's quite significant as far as our total production is concerned, and it's growing enormously

Three generations

every year. I've not travelled the world but I'm led to believe we are the lucky nation and it is fairly obvious we are. I think it's up to our parliamentarians to see it remains the lucky country. We don't have to import a heap of rubbish.'

Cliff's lack of travel experience is not a disappointment to him. 'After all, the world comes to us!' he laughs.

Cliff is now semi-retired and has handed management of the vineyard over to his son, Peter. Peter's wife, Jenny, handles the administration and their son, James, also works on the property. Cliff and Jean still live at their home, a stone's throw away from the cellars.

Life is a struggle for anyone who works on the land,

Cliff believes. Despite earning a comfortable existence from winemaking, he feels he only stopped struggling financially in the mid 1980s, after buying the company from the remainder of his family in 1982.

'Some people are fortunate enough to fall on their feet with a silver spoon but I don't believe they're any happier than those who battle and struggle. As a matter of fact, I don't think they appreciate life as much. At my age, I greet the morning by looking out the window. I see the cows come from the high country down to the low country, they've had their siesta at night and I've had mine. They wake up large and fresh, and I wake up and put my feet on the floor and say: "Well, there's another bonus!"'

PRESS PHOTOGRAPHER (RETIRED)

Point Lonsdale, Victoria

Born: Melbourne, Victoria, 1929

There is a story, more often a funny one, behind every one of the black and white photographs that line Clive MacKinnon's lounge room. Get him talking, and he can't help but share several of these stories with you, usually over several beers. Clive spent forty-six years as a newspaper photographer in Melbourne, covering every kind of news story there is, as well as every sport, including two Olympic Games. Regarded by his peers as brilliant and legendary, Clive established a reputation for mentoring younger photographers. He has witnessed, first hand, enormous changes in the media.

Clive retired in 1990, but recounts his favourite stories in such fresh and vivid detail, you'd think they happened yesterday. He even makes his own life sound like a news story. 'I was born on Melbourne Cup Day, the week the Depression started. Mum was a beautiful mother and my dad was a no-hoping drinker and gambler. All he wanted to do was drink grog, but he had a good job working for Shell which was an up-and-coming company. Dad's wages were four pounds a week. In the Depression, I can remember Mum hiding behind the door when the rent man came, because she didn't have the money to give him. People don't know what life was like for us.'

The greatest influence in Clive's life was his mother, Veenie, who he nursed at home prior to her death from cancer in 1971. 'My mum was the most beautiful sheila of all time. I think you inherit so much from your mother,' he says profoundly.

Clive joined the *Age* newspaper in 1946, intent on becoming a sports reporter. Instead he ended up in the photo department filing negatives, and was offered a cadetship as a photographer. 'I had to do a four-year cadetship and didn't even get a camera until I was there for two years. A cadet couldn't even go on a job on his own initiative because it was anti-union, and the pic editor wouldn't look at your photos.'

One of the first jobs Clive tagged along on with a senior photographer was the Head of the River rowing race in Geelong. 'I had a twelve-inch fixed-focus lens, and I only had one shot to get it right, with one plate in the camera. It was the closest boat race in history — the two boats went across the line together. I took this picture from the back of the ute and the students wouldn't keep still, so I reckon I was airborne when I took the photo. I was yelling at them to keep still. My photo was magnificent and the other guy didn't have a decent picture. I asked the boss if I could do a six-by-four of it for myself, and he refused. You weren't allowed to print or keep any of your shots then.'

Clive's confidence as a photographer grew quickly. 'I knew I was going to be a good photographer. I could beat the pants off most blokes I went out on a job with.

It wasn't me being a smart-arse, I just knew I was good at it. I was very fast, and I think I had a good newspaper sense. I think basically good photographers come out of being good newspaper men. It's changing now, because television has got us by the knackers. But up until the mid 1980s, there was still the ability for a man to express himself with a camera.'

Clive never had a mentor, and says he learned everything there was to know just by being on the job. He eventually began covering news events as well as sport, and early on, made a pact with himself about the pictures he shot. 'I took a stand that I wouldn't set up pictures. I would rather be scooped than set one up. All the pleasure of good pictures I've ever taken, not one of them has ever been set up. It's about recording the fair dinkum message. That's what's important about being a good photographer.'

Clive admits though, that like most press photographers, he was forced to compromise from time to time. 'When you go on jobs and there's nothing to make a picture — not a thing, NOTHING — then you have to create something. If the job was really important, you just had to get some sort of picture. No-one wanted to go back to the boss without one.'

After twenty-three years at the *Age*, Clive switched camps and went to work for the other major Melbourne newspaper, the *Sun News Pictorial*. The variety of life and the quality of people was what made the newspaper game so rewarding, yet at the same time so difficult for Clive. 'There were a lot of jobs you didn't want to do, where you had to share the sadness. There were people in dreadful situations and you had to go and try and talk to them. I would walk away and cry at jobs. I never got used to it, really,' he sighs.

'There was a man in South Australia in the 1983 Ash Wednesday bushfires and he asked his wife to take his four kids out of the danger area where the farm was. He stayed to fight the fire on the farm and off they went in the car and they all died, but he stayed safe on the farm. I went to his place the next day. You can imagine

the grief. God he was an heroic man. It was awful,' he says, his voice trembling. 'I often think of him now and wonder how he made out. He was a good bloke.'

Then there are the funnier moments, like when Clive covered the Moonee Valley races in the late 1980s. 'Before the race, you'd prepare your gear. You would pick your camera spot and put your gear down and knew no-one would touch it. You'd hang your camera on the fence. This particular day, I went to have a drink at the bar before the race. I knew my camera was ready. So, the horse — Kingston Town — goes past the post and Malcolm Johnston waves his whip and the camera goes bang and nothing happened. Some bastard had sabotaged me and turned my motor drive off. I knew who had done it though, and why.

'I knew Malcolm pretty well, and he came back to the scales elated, and I was down in the dumps and beaten. So I called out to him: "Malcolm, wave your whip". And he didn't quite hear me, so I yelled out again: "Wave your f***ing whip," and he went wild and his leg went up in the stirrups. I got a magnificent picture and I was the only one who got it!'

The days of old fashioned professional rivalry between newspaper photographers are over, Clive believes. 'I think everything is governed by money now. There are some great reporters and great photographers, but most of their work is going to be controlled by the dollar and the big business of TV and cross ownership. I don't think newspaper people are as fair dinkum as they used to be.'

HAT MAKER & ORGANIC FARMER

Mildura, Victoria

Born: Basel, Switzerland, 1950
& Mildura, Victoria, 1953

Hats of every shape, size, fabric and colour fill the back room of Krystyna Schweizer's home. Some are simple, some ornate, some defy description. The more elaborate hats are inspired by Krystyna's desire to make some kind of meaningful comment about the world. 'This is the John Howard sorry hat,' she says, picking up a velvet hat with a pair of hands extending from it. 'And here we have the Pauline Hanson hat — it has feathers and ribbons with all the colours of the world on it, displaying multiculturalism.'

Krystyna spends a few hours each day working on her hats. It is not a money-making business for her, but rather a therapeutic exercise in self-expression. Most of her time is consumed by caring for her eleven-year-old son Jesse, and helping her husband, Andrew Jones, run their organic farm. They are an unlikely couple. Krystyna is an energetic, spirited, creative and well-travelled woman and Andrew is a down-to-earth, softly spoken and relaxed third-generation farmer who has lived in the same place his whole life.

Krystyna grew up in Zaire. Her Swiss parents were Christian missionaries in villages where the locals had never seen a white person before. 'My parents didn't harm anyone, but in retrospect I thought what they were doing was taking away the local culture. I had three nannies and I spent more time with the indigenous people than with my parents.' By the age of seven, she spoke three African dialects, and by the time

she finished school, she spoke seven languages.

After training as a nurse in Switzerland, Krystyna came to Australia in 1971, responding to Australian government migrant recruitment publicity. She planned to spend two years here, treating it as a working holiday to learn English. On her arrival she found herself in a 'horrible hostel' in Sydney which she was not allowed to leave, so she and a girlfriend escaped by crawling along the floor below the receptionist's office, pushing their suitcases in front of them. She boarded a train to Melbourne and immediately found work at a nursing home.

Six months later, she was grape picking in Mildura when she met an Italian man, who she married the following year. They returned to Melbourne, where Krystyna worked in a community health centre. She had two daughters, Havale in 1973 and Naomi in 1974, but the marriage ended in 1978.

'I wasn't officially recognised as a nurse in Australia but I often got jobs as a medical receptionist because of my background. I interpreted a lot for Spanish, Italian, German and Turkish people. Doing this, I saw a lot of social welfare issues — I saw poverty and discrimination, and I wanted to be more active,' Krystyna recalls.

She decided to study social welfare, and moved to Darwin with her daughters. She almost completed the degree, but when she landed a job as a counsellor at an emergency accommodation centre in Mildura, she gave up the study and moved again. It was here she met Andrew Jones. They quickly struck up a relationship, and married in 1985.

Andrew had taken over running the sixty-acre family farm with his mother at the age of seventeen, after the death of his father. With Krystyna's heavy-handed prompting, Andrew converted from conventional to organic farming in the late 1980s. 'I had a compulsion to change the world, so poor Andrew got all the brainwashing about organic food and chemicals,' Krystyna laughs.

It was a three-year process for Andrew to get full

recognition as an organic grower from the National Association of Sustainable Agriculture of Australia. 'I hadn't sprayed insecticides for ten years before I switched,' Andrew explains. 'I had a conscience about it, but I was still using artificial fertilisers. It wasn't hard to convince me to switch. There were a lot of chemicals I didn't like using.'

Andrew grows a variety of table grapes as well as sultanas and currants, avocadoes, pumpkins, oranges and grapefruit. He is one of the few organic growers with a variety of dried food products. There are five organic growers in the Mildura area and they work in co-operation rather than in competition with each other.

The organic food market is on the rise again according to Andrew but it represents only a small percentage of the Australian market. 'Australia has a reputation for clean products anyway, which is why our market hasn't grown a lot, but with genetic modification of food coming in, I think there'll be a lot more interest in organic food now,' he says.

Andrew is convinced that organic farming is the best way to make farming land sustainable. 'It's produce coming from land that we can keep farming for generations to come. I went to Europe in 1990 and saw they're having major problems with chemicals in the ground. They haven't got a lot of hope in the future for producing a clean product. We can still use our rain water here, whereas they can't over there. If we don't do something, we'll end up like them too,' he explains.

Krystyna would like to see more government support for organic farmers. 'Here there is no incentive to grow organically, you actually get ridiculed as "new age greenies". It's not just about eating clean food, but about supporting the growers who make the decision to grow organically.' The benefits to the consumer, says Andrew, are quality for money, improved sense of taste and better health.

Andrew and Krystyna are hosts for Willing Workers On Organic Farms (WWOOF), a cultural exchange program giving visitors the opportunity to stay and work on an organic farm. Often they will have up to twenty WWOOF people staying with them.

Their son Jesse, born in 1988, was diagnosed with autism in 1997. He is highly intelligent and attends a normal school, but suffers from anxiety attacks and cannot cope with sudden changes. He has a photographic memory and is technically minded, but he is hyperactive and can be a danger to himself. At home, Krystyna needs to spend all her time with him. She started making hats to ease her anxiety and stress over Jesse's condition.

'In 1993 I went to Queensland to heal myself and someone mentioned the Maleny folk festival, so I took some hats along to try and sell them. I had no idea what my hats were — they had been just something else to focus on away from Jesse — but people went berserk over them at Maleny and I realised there was a market.

'I like hats with a theatrical flair, and how people can make an impression by wearing a hat. It gives you a sense of power. All chiefs in tribal society wear a headdress. I have worn so many hats, metaphorically speaking, in my life, I've had so many experiences and done so many different things and been involved in different causes, that all this repression exploded into hats. It had to come out somewhere!' she laughs loudly. 'Carl Jung would have had a field day!

'The townspeople think I'm totally insane, but it's a passion for me. It didn't start that way, it just grew. Every hat I make is part of me.

'My dream is to make hats an essential part of our attire again and to put hats back as ceremonial items because that's what missing in our lives: spirituality. It's almost like magic is attached to each hat.'

MUSICIAN
Killarney, Victoria
Born: Melbourne, Victoria, 1955

The audience is crammed into the Apollo Bay pub, waiting to hear Shane Howard, one of the first acts of the Apollo Bay Music Festival. Looking relaxed, but at the same time a little shy, Shane makes a few friendly exchanges with the distinctly older crowd as he waits for the house lights to dim.

'Sing "Flesh and Blood"!' a woman calls out.

'There's always one, isn't there,' he quickly retorts with a grin. It's clear he won't be singing that old favourite tonight — he has some newer songs, with a more important message, he wants to share instead.

Shane is a songwriter, guitarist, solo artist and the lead singer of Goanna, a band that found instant fame in 1982 with the song 'Solid Rock'. The band split in 1985, but reformed in 1998 and released a new album, *Spirit Returns*, in 1999. In between times, Shane has continued to write and record songs, but both his life and music have changed considerably.

Shane grew up in a musical household in the town of Warrnambool, on Victoria's southern coast. His three elder siblings and mother all played piano and they would sing together as a family at weddings, church services and CWA gatherings. 'We were the Howard family singers,' he says, smiling. 'We had to practise, so the discipline of that was always there. I thought this was going on in everyone's home. The house was a great centre for people who loved music — they always gravitated towards the place.'

When Shane's elder brother passed on his old guitar, Shane taught himself to play, writing his first song at the age of thirteen. His first solo public performance was a rendition of 'Blowing in the Wind' at a school concert.

Bob Dylan was a key influence on Shane, along with Van Morrison, Joni Mitchell and Neil Young. 'They're the four that have really remained true to their art. But I have to say Dylan was the biggest influence. He sets the benchmark for me, as a writer. He is the song poet laureate of the twentieth century. He gave all songwriters a career — serious writing in pop music didn't exist before him. It's important historically because he created a place for the singer–songwriter.'

Australian musical influences were non-existent until Shane went to the Sunbury Music Festival in 1972, and saw a band called Country Radio. 'They were one of the first bands in Australia to write about Australian subject matter and to do folk rock music,' he says. 'They blew my mind. Here for the first time was an Australian band playing something other than rock and roll, and they were lyrical.

'No-one was really saying what I wanted to hear because there were no Australian songwriters. I was motivated to write about my own situation. When you've lived all your life in a little country town, this stuff was big.'

By 1976, Shane was living in Geelong and had formed a band which played the pub circuit for the next two years. When singer Rose Bygrave joined the group in 1979, the line-up changed, and the new band, Goanna, began making inroads into Melbourne and regional Victoria, building up a decent following.

In 1981, Goanna was scouted by Warner Brothers when it was the support act for the national James Taylor tour. 'The next thing we knew we were making a record, which was *Spirit of Place*. Then the very first song we put out, "Solid Rock", went to number one in the summer of 1982. The record company thought this song was doomed to failure because it was too political and heavy. We felt very strongly about the fact it should be the first comment we made, and we thought we'd get a bit of airplay, but next thing you know it's on every time you turn on the radio.

' "Solid Rock" was significant in that it was one of the first commercial pop songs to address the subject of Aboriginal land rights. I don't know why the spirit moved, but it did and it said this song is going to affect Australian consciousness. Some songs come from you and some songs come through you. "Solid Rock" came through me.'

In retrospect however, Shane still wonders how many people heard the true message in 'Solid Rock'. 'It sold well because it had a beat and you could dance to it. It had a didgeridoo, the iconography was really Australian, but you see, no-one sang about Australia at the time. Apart from The Dingoes and Country Radio, no-one sang about what it was like to live in Australia — they sang about Pasadena or Hollywood. I don't think an Aboriginal singing a song like "Solid Rock" would have gotten through at that time. It was another ten years before you saw an Aboriginal band come up through the mainstream.'

Shane says he was dissatisfied with the impact of the song when he toured and saw the extent of racism in Australia. 'Every little town we went to there'd be at least half a dozen Aboriginal people coming to our shows, wondering who these whitefellas who were singing about their country, and every night after the show, we'd sit down and talk to all these people.'

Shane wrote 'Solid Rock' after a trip to Uluru in 1980. 'The first night I was there, I had cooked up a feed and I was sitting there playing guitar. It was an amazing sight, the rock. It has this awesome presence and energy that surrounds it. Then this wave hit me. I sobbed uncontrollably for about twenty minutes. Something overpowered me. I didn't understand what it was. The next day I asked permission from the community to go places. I witnessed a traditional corroboree that night. As the first dancer came into the circle, the full moon rose. It was like an awakening to the fact that here was this incredibly sophisticated culture in the desert. I was totally humbled by the experience and their spiritual power and presence.

'My own experience had been of very colonised, disempowered Aboriginal people, and all of a sudden what I'd read in terms of their mythology was alive and real. I went back to Alice Springs and saw the decimation caused by colonisation and what a contrast it was. The disempowerment that colonisation has caused for Aboriginal people has never left me.'

Following the success of 'Solid Rock', Goanna toured nationally and in the USA, but they never had another hit song. In 1985, the band broke up, as did Shane's marriage of ten years.

'It was a consequence of too much too soon,' says Shane, 'and the other aspect was seeing the corporate reality of a greedy world, and the fact that business has no morality. The thing that disempowered Aboriginal people was the same thing that disempowered us. Essentially it was greed. All this just sharpened my social criticism.' For the next eight years Shane 'went bush', living in Broome, Cairns and Kuranda. He continued to write songs, but performing took a back seat.

Writing music comes instinctively to Shane, but it is still something he has to make time to do. 'I've learned that if something wants to be written, you just do it. There are little moments of insight you have and I guess the discipline is learning to recognise those insights. The real work then is to flesh something out to a wholeness, and that's hard work.'

In addition to a successful solo career throughout the 1990s, Shane produced a number of albums by other Australian artists, including The Pigram Brothers' *Saltwater Country* and Andy Albert's *Gunditjmara Land*. After touring with Irish singer Mary Black in 1992, Shane visited Ireland in 1993 and discovered some of his Irish ancestry. Mary's recording of Shane's song 'Flesh and Blood' in 1993 was a top-five hit and she has since recorded a number of his tunes.

Shane's most recent album, *Clan*, consolidates his reputation as a commentator on indigenous rights and social justice. His life philosophy, clearly evident in so much of his music, is: 'Everyone is equal. No-one has the right to place themselves above anyone.'

COLOUR THERAPIST/ HEALER

Walwa, Victoria

Born: Geelong, Victoria, 1948

The long, steep and bumpy driveway to Barbara Pritchard's home winds its way up a mountainside overlooking the Murray River. Her simple stone bungalow, its frame built from gumtree branches, is tucked away in the lush green grass at the top. The doorless outdoor dunny has a lovely view over the creek that flows beside the house. There is privacy, simplicity, natural beauty and a sense of serenity here.

When Barbara first arrived on this land in 1984, she lived with her three sons — then aged two, four and six — in a caravan without power or running water. 'Life was really hard. I did my washing in the creek, and used gas and candles for lights. Once a storm came and blew the dunny away!'

Barbara first came to Walwa in 1978 with her husband, a doctor, who set up a practice in the town. They broke up in 1982, and Barbara bought the mountain-top land two years later.

Barbara's combined bathroom and laundry is filled with brightly coloured pieces of silk in the process of being dyed. They will be used later for colour therapy, a technique for healing people, emotionally and physically, through the use of colour. Barbara spent twenty years working as a nurse and midwife, always believing in her own ability to facilitate healing. She also had talent as an artist, and painted regularly. When she discovered she had an unusual gift, her career and life changed direction.

'I started seeing energy fields around patients,' Barbara explains, 'so I decided to stop nursing and go towards art. Prior to this I had been producing work for exhibitions at different galleries around the place. In 1991 I opened a gallery of painted silk scarves, which was when I realised my art and healing could be matched

together. People visiting the gallery were relating the colours to their emotions, saying, "this makes me feel good", or "that feels awful". Some people would walk into the room and I could see their colours change. I could see how colours were profoundly affecting their energy fields, so I built on this.'

In 1994 Barbara held an exhibition called 'Healing Art', and presented the concept of using colour in healing at the first holistic nurses conference in Perth. For her colour therapy work, Barbara makes scarves and garments from hand-dyed silks, using thirty-nine colours. Each of these colours has a different impact on a person emotionally — for example, blue is a good colour for communicating, red is a grounding colour. These clothes are sold with explanatory labels to shops. Barbara also uses the fabrics in personal counselling.

'In a session, I take a life history and date of birth to get a numbers vibration. Then I put them on a table and assess their energy field. I give different kinds of treatment depending on people's needs. I work on putting colours on their energy fields. I put the colours in a certain sequence and I'll get directions as to how many times to wave a certain colour over their body. Once you start dealing with energy fields, then the earth starts giving you a lot more information, because the earth is the great healer. I was taught earth wisdom on trips overseas with indigenous people from Australia and New Zealand.' Earth wisdom, according to Barbara, is the ancient knowledge and spiritual practices of indigenous people which is used in healing.

Barbara stresses that she only facilitates peoples' healing through her work. 'It's about people taking responsibility for their own healing. When they're ready for healing, then they come to a healer.' Her methods have been more quickly accepted in the USA, where she has taught the concept in Cincinatti, Atlanta and Hawaii. 'The Americans are very visionary people and they take on board new concepts easily. It's because they've made their own way so much more and they open themselves up to new ideas and new ways. Australians aren't as quick to pick up on new ideas. There's the sense of domination from Britain. It's in our psyche, we've never been able to create a vision for ourselves.'

Barbara believes mainstream medicine is changing its attitude to alternative treatments, albeit slowly. 'The medical profession is opening up to different modalities and other holistic ways of healing. That's why I think colour therapies are being adopted so readily. It's about sensitising practitioners to how powerful it is. They already use a kind of colour therapy with psychotic people to calm down violent behaviour.'

It was her nursing experience that gave Barbara an insight into the potential power of people to heal, but she feels a nurse's intuition is often overlooked. 'Our observations of patients were dismissed as being unimportant by the hierarchy, and yet it's the small observations that are important. There are people who have a healing presence — their actual being there helps the person. It's a big issue that nurses are leaving the

profession in droves these days, because the care is being taken away from the bedside. No longer is there the healing touch of the nurse. I think the education of nurses is really good at the moment, but somewhere along the line, the nurse has to be brought back to the essential contact with the person who's ill.'

With interest in her field growing rapidly, Barbara

has plans to build a studio and run teaching workshops on her property. She and her husband Neil, an electrician, hope to complete a mud-brick house and turn their bungalow into visitor accommodation for people attending the workshops. 'I think Americans would benefit a lot from coming here to stay; they'd find it interesting. An American woman once told me I should run "wild women" workshops because I lived in the bush!' she laughs.

She is not surprised at the speed with which her new business has taken off. 'I'm a bit of believer that if you stick at something long enough, you will be successful. Success to me is feeling really good in your heart, it's not about the car you drive or the house you live in.'

CAFE PROPRIETORS

Allans Flat, Victoria

Born: Bolzano, Italy, 1943 & Monk, Austria, 1952

A pine chalet sits on a quiet road through the Yackandandah Valley, about six kilometres east of the historic town. 'Viennese Patisserie', the sign out the front says, beckoning tourists who don't expect much more than tea and scones in this neck of the woods. With Austrian accordion music playing, Walter chats with customers on the verandah as he takes orders for coffee and cake. Inside, Waltraud serves up her traditional tortes and handmade chocolates.

Walter and Waltraud Moroso first saw Australia in 1984 when they spent three months travelling the country and debating the pros and cons of emigrating to the great southern land. They kept separate diaries to record their feelings about Australia but it wasn't until they returned to Europe that they discovered their desire to make a fresh start in a new country was completely mutual.

Walter, an industrial engineer, had been working in Germany and felt stressed in his career. In the 1980s, he designed, built and raced motorcycles, developing his own brand of racing bike. Waltraud, a pastry chef, was searching for a change of scene and a secure place to raise their then sixteen-month-old son, Marco, and Andrea, her sixteen-year-old daughter from a previous marriage.

'We wanted to find a new life in an environment which would give us a better life for our children in an open-minded country,' explains Walter. 'We are different settlers from the ones who came here between 1955 and 1960. They escaped from troublesome Europe after the war. We are the generation things were going well for, so we didn't really have a good reason to leave. But we wanted more freedom of life, and Australia had what we were looking for.'

After making inquiries at the Frankfurt office for business immigrants to Australia, the couple arrived in Melbourne in 1985, intent on pursuing their dream of setting up a small business, an authentic Austrian patisserie, somewhere in north-eastern Victoria. But before buying land on which to build the cafe, they planned to familiarise themselves with the area and earn a living from Walter's industrial skills.

'We arrived with a forty-foot container with my entire workshop in it,' Walter recalls. 'Then we rented a business in Wodonga and I put a sign on the door saying, "Small or big cheques, everything accepted." All these people came in and trusted me and gave me jobs. I did a range of fibreglass jobs — fixing boats, cars and aeroplanes.'

Still grateful to the customers who helped him earn a living in those first few years in a new country, Walter says there was never a time when he didn't feel accepted. 'I reckon Australia is the friendliest, most inviting country in the world when it comes to adjustment and acceptance,' he says emphatically.

Waltraud is quick to agree. 'I think nowhere else in the world would you be accepted so quickly. Perhaps in America, but certainly not in Europe.'

In 1987 the couple bought ten acres in Allans Flat, a rural area just south of the New South Wales–Victorian border. 'There was absolutely nothing on the land when we came here,' Waltraud recalls. 'Everything you see around you, we put here.' The family of four lived in a campervan for two-and-a-half years while Walter built a large shed, which then housed the family for another three years while he built the home.

The cafe, a typical mountain chalet, is built from pine taken from the timber mills at nearby Myrtleford and Stanley. Walter suffered two hernias while lifting the pine beams, but continued to work. Although some people thought them mad to choose a relatively remote place for such a business, the Morosos had faith that it would work. Situated close to a number of historic towns in the north-east corner of Victoria, they were counting on a consistent tourist population travelling through the area to keep the business viable.

The cafe opened in December 1995 and since then business has been steady. Waltraud's day begins at 6 am, when she starts baking cakes and pastries in her home. She learned her craft at a cooking school in Vienna, and never uses artificial ingredients. Some of her cake recipes are 300 years old. 'I love to cook and I love good food and I think as long as we're healthy, we're happy too. I don't worry about work. I like to work where I live. My philosophy is, why shouldn't you work and live where you like to live?'

Waltraud encourages their son Marco to help in the cafe. 'I want to teach him about life, that you have to work hard to earn what you want. A lot of people think life is so easy and look for hand-outs, but I think you bring your own luck in life. We are hard workers, but we don't see it as work. We don't think about how difficult it is. We work hard but we don't forget how to enjoy life either. We have very good friends we've made through the multicultural society, and we get together and have good meals. We have a whole mix of friends. Our attitude about people is that it's about people, not their colour.'

Walter adds: 'In Europe, prejudice was a major part of life and we wanted to get away from it. I think if Australia was a narrow-minded country we wouldn't be here.'

Each July, Walter and Waltraud go on a month's holiday, but they're always happy to return home. 'Once a year we go to Merimbula for a week, but I'm glad to come back. One week by the sea is enough. I love the challenge of the different seasons here,' says Walter.

'You pay the price for the environment you choose. We don't make so much money by living here, but we have a beautiful lifestyle. If every day you get up and your first thought is: Not another day in the office with ugly people around me that make my life hard, then this is one of the worst feelings you can have as a human being! When I get up here, I look out the window and say, "Another beautiful day, sunshine, blue sky, and a business I really love to do."'

RETIRED LOGGER
Mengha, Tasmania
Born: Melbourne, Victoria, 1928

Brian Stone's home, tucked away on a remote 35-acre property in north-west Tasmania, sits adjacent to a Tasmanian forestry site. Whichever way he looks, Brian is surrounded by trees — some felled and cleared, some thick and fully grown, some just beginning to grow again. It's much like the view Brian had every working day for forty years in his job as a logging contractor.

Until 1991 Brian worked in the Tasmanian forests as a contractor responsible for the felling, barking, loading and transport of timber. Brian and his wife Mary moved from the north-west town of Smithton to Mengha in 1994 to retire, but Brian is more active now than ever. In preparation for what he describes as 'massive earth changes', which he believes will occur in the near future, Brian is now working towards complete self-sufficiency.

He installed solar power, is building a wind-powered generator, and has a substantial vegetable garden. His kitchen has a wood-fired stove, and his sheds are crammed with tools and the assorted equipment necessary to fend for oneself. Brian's belief in these earth changes developed after he overcame throat cancer in 1985 through natural therapies.

'When I came out of hospital, I read a book called *A World Without Cancer*, by G. Edward Griffin, which made me aware of all this. It opened me up to the cartels — pharmaceuticals, petrochemicals, the banks. It was the most startling thing I'd ever read. Before this, I thought governments were honest. I was just living in the mainstream and believed everything I was told in the news, but then I took my life into my own hands.'

Since 1994 Brian has spent a couple of hours each day researching theories on earth changes and world conspiracies. He reads little-known international magazines like Gordon Michael Scallion's *Earth Changes*, which predict major geographical changes to the earth.

'It's quite evident to me what's going to happen. We're warming up. The environmental scientists will tell you the seas are dead. Look at Bangladesh, it's part underwater already. We're going through different ages — planet earth goes through a grand cycle of 26,000 years. We are right on a change now. These changes will bury the cartels. We could get massive solar flares which would cause a magnetic pole shift and take all our technology away.'

'I reckon everything will happen in the next thirteen years. I would have gone and lived on the Arthur River but anything at sea level won't be safe, which is why I've ended up here, being self-sufficient. If we do lose our technology, I've got three families with my grandchildren all ready to come out and live here. We have water, we can grow food, and we have plenty of wood for power.'

Brian is convinced his life-threatening illness was the beginning of his 'awakening', and that up until then, he had wasted his life. 'I could have made better use of my life if I'd been aware of all the things I know now. I had the best opportunities but I wasted them.'

Despite his new-found environmental consciousness, Brian does not carry any guilt about his career as a timber getter. 'I do know the logging's going to have to stop, and I know now we shouldn't have done it. We've just devastated the planet and taken away its oxygen.'

Brian's introduction to the timber industry came in 1946, when he started as a mechanic at the Lee and Sons sawmill in Smithton, which employed about 300 people.

By 1952 Brian had bought his own truck and got his first contract with a sawmill as a log carter. 'I carted up until 1961, then I got my first full logging contract with Lee and Sons to fell, load, bark and deliver the logs to their sawmill.' An ordinary day for Brian meant leaving home at 6 am and travelling for an hour or so to reach the logging site. He would take the feller, dozer operator and barker with him. 'I was given a quota that I had to meet each day. It was very stressful with all the machinery involved and regular breakdowns, and the weather being a hazard.' The work was also physically demanding and often dangerous. The most serious injury Brian witnessed in his logging career was his own. In 1976 he lost most of his index finger when it got caught in the fan of a bulldozer's engine.

For ten years, Brian logged selectively in areas allocated by the Tasmanian Forestry Commission, but when the first woodchip mill was built on the Tamar River in 1967, clear felling — clearing an entire section of forest — was introduced. 'After '71 they took everything. Before that we were only getting hardwood, blackwood, myrtle, leatherwood, celery and sassafras.'

By 1975 Brian had twenty-nine men working for him. It was the year the Green movement, led by Dr Bob Brown, gained momentum and the logging protests began. 'I never clashed with protestors, they weren't ever on our end of the island. I was aware of the protests, but I never gave them much thought.'

Australia's environmental consciousness, especially in terms of logging, is reasonably healthy, Brian believes. 'I think Australia is the best in the world as far as replantation goes, but they're not planting enough different species of tree.'

Brian sold his business in 1991 and spent three years running a timber yard in Smithton before retiring. Looking remarkably fit and younger than his years, Brian's outlook on life is fresh, yet there is a sense of urgency when he speaks about the future. 'I feel the most motivated and the most positive I have in my whole life. 'But you've got to make others aware of what might happen. Make no mistake, these earth changes are coming. I don't want to put fear into people, I just want to make them aware so they'll prepare. We have to make a better future for our children.'

CHEESE-MAKER

Elizabeth Town, Tasmania

Born: Devonport, Tasmania, 1969

Mounds of maturing cheese are stacked high, row after row, in the cooling room at Jane Bennett's farm-based cheese factory. As she labels wedges of cheese in an adjoining packing room late on a Saturday afternoon, Jane's uncle, John, is rounding up the cows for milking, and her father, Michael, is attending to customers in the factory shop.

Ashgrove Farm Cheese is a family-run business, but it is Jane who clearly has the authority when it comes to making cheese. Ironically, it was never a career Jane envisaged for herself. 'I spent my school holidays working on the farm because it was easier than picking fruit, which was the alternative. It was easier to drive the tractor than pick raspberries or strawberries,' she begins.

'I was going to go off to uni to do teaching, but it wasn't until my last term in Grade Twelve that I realised I didn't want to do it. I didn't know what I wanted to do, but I knew I quite liked being on the farm and living in the country. It never occurred to me until then that it was a career option for me to come back to the farm.'

John was president of the Australian Dairy Farmers Federation for eleven years, until the mid 1980s, and also deputy chair of the Australian Dairy Corporation during a period of great change in the industry. Jane says it was her uncle's knowledge and concern about dairy commodity prices on the world market that led to the decision to make cheese, although it was her father

Michael who suggested, less than subtly, that Jane should take it up.

'It was never my intention to be a cheese-maker and I don't think any teenager who hadn't been brought up in an environment of cheese-making would contemplate it as a career option. It certainly had absolutely ZERO appeal to me. It was Dad who was just so obsessed with this bloody cheese-making. He had a dream, he wanted to see a cheese factory here, and I just happened to be the means to an end. He said to me: "You've got to be a cheese-maker, you can do it."'

Persuaded, Jane opted to do a two-year college course in dairy production but, despite her farm experience, went in feeling totally unprepared. 'I had no knowledge of dairy. I knew that you put a cup on a teat and the milk came out,' she laughs. 'When I got to college, I was the only girl in class of eighteen and the only student who didn't work in the dairy industry. The

dairy companies were sending their staff to the college and there was this expectation of a base knowledge and everybody else had this, except for me. I didn't even know what a pasteuriser was, let alone what it did.'

After successfully completing her course, Jane was rewarded with a trip to England, the result of a deal she had done with her dad two years earlier. She planned to learn how to make English-style cheeses. 'All I had was the names of two people who made cheese. I went to Lancashire and these people offered to give me a try. I intended to stay two months and stayed for eighteen. When I wrote home and told Dad they wanted to keep me for five years, Dad faxed me back this auction catalogue for a dairy factory asking what he should buy, then he went off and bought all this cheese-making equipment.'

Jane returned home in 1992 and began making cheese in December 1993. Her father and uncle had

no say in the kind of cheese they would produce. 'I knew how to make English-style cheese, so I said: "Okay, you're going to get English-style cheeses." We knew we had to make hard cheese because we don't milk the cows all year round here, and we needed something that would keep for a long period of time. We also knew we were not going to be able to compete with other Australian cheese-makers and make something they were already making, so the idea for us was to be an import replacement company.'

At the time, Jane found her confidence boosted by the negative opinions of those around her. The market researchers told her she we would never sell English-style cheeses in Australia, estimating she would only sell six tonnes a year nationally.

'Nobody took us seriously when we said we were going to make cheese. I'm the sort of dreadful person who is inspired by those with cynicism. I love to prove them wrong,' she smiles. 'We ignored all the best marketing advice we were given and produced not only English-style cheese, but also Lancashire. People asked me why I would make it and I said: "Because it's my favourite style cheese and I don't care if nobody else eats it, I'll have some!"'

By 1999, the company was selling 130 tonnes of cheese per year, with Lancashire one of the strongest sellers. Jane makes nine kinds of traditional English cheese, which has to be graded by people from England because there is no-one in Australia qualified to do it.

'I think all you need to do weird and wonderful things is for someone to have a belief in you, and Dad and John had that belief in me. The first day I made cheese I was terrified. I had no back-up — the nearest back-up was in the UK, I was using equipment that was a mish-mash of stuff I'd never used before. It was only their faith in me that made me think: maybe I can do it. It was never my dream to develop this — it was really Dad and John's dream. But to go out there into the cool room and see all those cheeses and think: "Wow I made all this." Well, then I think perhaps I have been a bit productive.'

Now a great enthusiast of the dairy industry, Jane is actively involved with the administrative side of things. She is the chair of the Tasmanian Rural Industry Training Board, which co-ordinates training within the industry. 'When I was invited to take this position, I was the first female to chair it and the youngest by about twenty years, but I thought: "Bugger it, I've probably got more brains than most of these blokes."'

Drawing on her own childhood experience, Jane saw the need for training as vital. "I was brought up on a farm where nobody taught you anything, they just yelled at you to do it and you had to know how, even though you'd never been shown,' she explains. 'I had never started the tractor and one time we were down in the paddock and Dad yelled I had to take the tractor back to the shearing shed and he just took off. I had steered it and stopped it before, but never started it. He came steaming back and I had to tell him I couldn't start it. So I was very much aware there is a great need for training and that our industry won't survive unless we're educated and pass on our knowledge.'

In 1997, Jane's success earned her the title of Rural Woman of the Year. Since then, she has become much busier, attending rural business functions as well as being in demand as a speaker. She continues to make cheese six days a week, and says her social life is atrocious. Jane's own diet isn't entirely supportive of the industry on which she thrives. She eats cheese and loves ice cream, but she hates milk and never eats butter.

SNAKE-HANDLER
Taranna, Tasmania
Born: Campbelltown, Tasmania, 1963

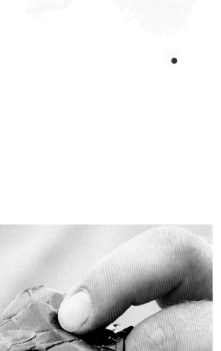

A thick black snake slithering around his forearm, Smiley stands firm but relaxed in the centre of the circular snake pit, surrounded by hundreds of the creatures. One of the snakes has just given birth, and Smiley grabs a ten centimetre long newborn from the grass, looking around for the other twenty or so that were born with it. The babies must be separated from the adults before most of them get eaten.

'These babies are like caviar to us, they're absolutely beautiful,' Smiley tells his small but fascinated audience. 'They shed their skins when they're ten minutes old and it's in their nature to attack from the moment they're born.' An earthy, good-natured bloke, Smiley has been the snake handler and manager of the World Tiger Snake Centre at Taranna, on the Tasman Peninsula, since it first opened at the end of 1996. Tiger snakes are being bred at the centre for medical research by a syndicate of scientists in Sydney, Melbourne and Adelaide.

Smiley fell into snake-handling by accident. He had been working in an abattoir on King Island, one of a group of islands in Bass Strait populated by large numbers of tiger snakes. 'These snakes were up the other end of it [the island] and this bus load of tourists came in one day and wanted to see them, and I was the only one there who would do it. They wanted to know what I knew about them and wanted me to pick one up, so I got in there and picked up the fattest

snake I could because I thought he'd be really slow, and I've been at it ever since.'

Smiley was soon offered a job by Dick Lawrence, a livestock breeder and snake-handler from Cressy, who had previously visited King Island collecting snakes for the first tiger-snake breeding program. Up to this point, Smiley's life experience had already been quite broad, having worked as a fettler for the Tasmanian railways for fourteen years and prior to this, as a tree barker in the midland forests.

Smiley's father left when he was a toddler, leaving his mother to raise six children on her own. 'I had a hard childhood, we did everything hard. I was brought up the old way and taught to respect my elders. We lived off the land, and caught fish and game. We had chooks and ducks. In the early days we had our own milking cow and we made our own butter. If I was ever out of work now,' he adds as an afterthought, 'I'd never starve.'

Although he enjoyed his job at the abattoir, Smiley relished the opportunity to work with snakes because of their unique potential for medical research. 'The research is going so well it's not funny. The scientists are rapt about how things are going. All the big medical companies are sitting up, waiting and listening.

'They're trying to come up with one antivenene to cover all snake bites by using their venom, and in their blood, there could be a cure for some forms of cancer, arthritis and asthma. That's the only reason I'm doing this job. This is far too dangerous a job to be doing it just for the tourism. If we come up with a cure for one of these three things, then I've done my bit in life.'

The tiger snake is the fourth deadliest snake in the world after the fierce, the inland taipan and the brown, but Smiley has no fear. 'The first time my mother saw me work with the snakes, she went off her head. It's bred into us to be scared of snakes. Now and then they'll startle you, but if I feared them I wouldn't be working with them. If it was an octopus or spider, you wouldn't

see me anywhere near it. We don't need anything with more than four legs in this world!' he laughs.

Smiley estimates he's been bitten thirty times in his snake-handling career. Ironically, he refuses to take antivenene and won't give the doctors any of his blood for testing, because he's terrified of needles. When he gets bitten, he chooses to ride out the effects, which, for tiger snakebite, can be different each time.

'One day I got bitten, and I came home that night alone. I started throwing up, I was in and out of consciousness and bleeding out of my nose and ears. When my lungs started to tighten, I thought I'd better call an ambulance. I woke up by the phone the next morning because I'd lapsed into unconsciousness. I'm only pushing my luck, I'm really pushing it,' he says seriously, yet still grinning. 'For me, to get a bank loan is near impossible — I'm in the high-risk category!'

Smiley is building a house with his fiance, who works at a nearby bakery and as a tour guide at the historic penal settlement of Port Arthur. The Snake Centre was in fact established close to Port Arthur in an effort to bring tourists back to the area, after the tragedy in April 1995 when thirty-five people died at the historic site.

Although he plans to make Tasmania home for the rest of his life, Smiley is deeply concerned about his state. 'Tasmania is the only state in Australia where the population is decreasing yearly. Five thousand people left here in 1998. You can buy a reasonable three- or four-bedroom house for $150,000 here and get three acres with it, but every second house is for sale. There's no work here. They say they're going to create all these new jobs but the mainland gets all the work.

'The biggest problem with Tasmania today is that everyone wants to get rich really quick. I was born a worker, and to me it's against my religion to see people getting ripped off. For a mum and dad and two kids to come out of Hobart for a day and do everything on the Peninsula, they get no change out of $200. People can't afford it anymore. Tassie is a good little island but all the government wants to do is rip the working man off.

'As for myself, I'm glad the government has no say on these snakes, because they're privately owned. I just hope that once they make the drugs they need then the centre will be open to the public free of charge.'

SHIP'S CAPTAIN
Devonport, Tasmania
Born: Sydney, New South Wales, 1945

John Hadley

It is dawn, and as the *Spirit of Tasmania* cruises towards the Port of Melbourne, Captain John Hadley is eating breakfast in his quarters. The overnight sail from Devonport across Bass Strait has been a smooth and uneventful one. Shortly, John will go up to the bridge and remain there for the final hour of this very familiar journey as he calmly guides the vessel into the dock. He does this six times a week: three into the Port of Melbourne, three into Devonport.

The Captain's quarters are much like a good hotel room: not plush, not opulent, just comfortable and functional. On this level, you can feel the swell as just a mere sway. Four decks below, the passengers are emerging from their cabins as they prepare to embark. Even further below, others are getting into their cars and campervans, ready to drive out of the bowels of the boat.

The *Spirit* is the major means of transport to Tasmania for most tourists. It has 459 cabins, carries up to 1,300 passengers, and has the capacity for 355 cars and fifty-five semi-trailers. Setting sail from Devonport at 6 pm, it arrives in Melbourne by 8.30 am the following morning.

John doesn't allow himself to be overwhelmed by the responsibility of safely 'parking' 31,356 tonnes of steel, 180 metres in length. 'Getting the ship in and out doesn't feel stressful to me — it's not something I worry about — but the risks are limitless. If you actually sat down

and figured out all the risks, you wouldn't do it. It involves a lot of concentration in a short period of time.'

John has been captaining the *Spirit* since 1997, and has spent his career on ships around the world. Like father, like son — his father, who is now in his eighties, captained the *Princess of Tasmania* in Bass Strait from 1959 to 1981.

'I'd love a dollar for every time I've been asked why I went to sea. From the time I was twelve years old, I always intended going to sea because my father went to sea. He never mentioned it or forced me into it, but I never assumed I was going to do anything else.

'I never went through the "what will I do" phase. We went off to see the careers adviser and he asked me what I had in mind. I said I was going to sea, so he spent the rest of the interview telling me I couldn't do that in Australia. I told him I certainly could, then he went off and found out how you did it.'

John started as a cadet in 1962, working his way through the various maritime certificates necessary to move up in the world of shipping. He earned his master's licence in 1971 and became master of a ship for the first time in 1979. 'That was really the genesis of being here, because I was one of the traders that consistently did the Bass Strait run on the cargo ships.'

In the 1980s John worked between Australia and Japan on the *Australian Emblem*. Between 1989 and 1994, he captained the *Australian Sea Road*, a car-carrier vessel which went world tramping. After a few years doing the Europe run on the *Australian Venture*, he secured the job on the *Spirit*. 'The *Spirit* is completely different from anything I've ever done before. There's still the bringing it in and bringing it out, but it's mainly administrative,' he says.

John chose to leave his Sydney home at the age of twenty and live in Hobart because of its proximity to the airport and the shipping port. 'I lived in Sandy Bay, which was just vacant hills at first. Now it's all houses. But if you go down the main street of Hobart, it actually hasn't changed much at all, apart from the fact that

there used to be two restaurants to go to, and now there are hundreds.'

Hobart, says John, is still regional Australia. 'It's not a city.' Tasmania's falling population, he believes, is 'pretty typical' of all regional centres throughout the country. 'Tasmania is a major tourist destination and has massive potential for tourism, but I personally believe it should be run as one big company,' he says earnestly.

'It would work better, because Tasmanians are what you call your genuine conservatives. They don't like change, so they embrace things like the Greens movement very quickly; not because they're conservationists but because they don't like change, so anybody who says "don't change this" gets masses of support.

'A classic example is when they wanted to put a cable car up Mount Wellington, and there was all this business that it would destroy the city, yet all you'd see is a cable car. Nobody knows exactly why they were opposed to it — all they could say was that it wasn't there before so they didn't want it there now.'

In summer, John also pilots the high-speed *Devil Cat*, a catamaran which takes six hours to cross Bass Strait. He spends a month on the *Spirit* then a month on the *Cat*. 'Driving the two is like chalk and cheese. The *Cat* has been good for tourism. I think anything that brings people into Tassie is good.'

APIARIST
Mole Creek, Tasmania
Born: Mole Creek, Tasmania, 1930

A plain red brick building is crowned by distant lush green hills. Fading yellow letters above its doors say 'Golden Bee' and 'Golden Nectar'. In the green field next door, crouching down among the yellow daisies, Ian Stephens, his face netted for safety, is checking a stack of hives using the traditional method of smoking to tranquillise the bees.

Ian has handled bees ever since he can remember. As a child, he would rather spend time with the bees than go to school. His father Robert, who started out as a hobby beekeeper in 1914, returned from the war in 1918 to establish a honey production plant in the mid-northern town of Mole Creek. Twelve years later — the same year Ian was born — the red brick building went up and he established the now internationally recognised Golden Bee and Golden Nectar trademarks for his honey.

A strange sense of timelessness hovers here: the way Ian goes about his work, the bees buzzing round his face, the simple labels on the honey jars, the building itself. An elderly couple pull up at the building, get their honey tin out of the car boot and take it inside to be refilled. It could still be the 1960s.

In fact the only things that have really changed about the place in almost seventy years, Ian believes, are the mechanisation and bottling procedures. 'We got it right in the first place, so there's no point changing it,' he says matter-of-factly. It was, he explains, his father's

bee-breeding experiments, as well as being in the ideal location, that resulted in the right formula for their leatherwood, clover and blackberry honeys.

'In the 1920s Dad crossed two kinds of bee: the English Black and the Yellow Italian Green. It was the first cross of its kind and no-one else has done it since. We've got the same kind of bees we had in 1925, and we still work the same way. My bees have a wider wing span and a bigger body so they fly further and carry more honey. Eventually it will be recognised as a new race of bee, but it's only now just starting to be recognised by other beekeepers worldwide. In the next five years, it should finally have a name of its own.'

Tasmanian honey has a long-standing reputation for being the best in the world. Tasmania is the world's only source of leatherwood honey, and the leatherwood tree (*Eucryphia lucida* and *Eucryphia milliganii*) only grows in

the western half of the state in pristine rainforest areas, many of them listed as World Heritage sites. Tasmanian leatherwood hives produce about 600 tonnes of honey annually, half of which is exported.

Every January, when the leatherwood is in flower, Ian transports his hives to rainforest areas on the west coast. In the three months prior to this, the hives have to be inspected every fourteen days to ensure they are disease free and the queen is in good condition. The leatherwood flowers for just eight to ten weeks, and each hive produces about sixty kilograms of honey.

In 1966, after serving a long apprenticeship, Ian took over the business from his father and expanded it commercially. Presently the market leader in Tasmania, Ian's factory now produces 300 tonnes of honey a year, all of which is sold in advance. He produces thirty-five per cent of the honey in Tasmania from fourteen per

cent of the total number of hives. His annual turnover is $1 million. About eighteen per cent of Ian's product is sold within Tasmania, fifty per cent goes to the mainland, and the remainder is exported to such countries as the USA, Greece, Lebanon, Malaysia, Singapore and England.

Confident in the knowledge that his product is of the highest quality, Ian still holds fast to the basic business philosophy his father taught him. 'You have to have a quality product. A good-quality product has a market anywhere in the world. My father always said that you should sell something at the same price to everyone, and it's worked very well over the years, especially with export. I said to some Japanese buyers recently, "When you've got enough money, then come back and see me", because they didn't want to pay the price I was asking.

'If you sell anything to the public, you have to be spot on with the product, then you can demand the price you want. I maintain my honey is the best, so I should get top price.' Ian's honey retails for about a dollar a jar more than most commercial brands. What gives him the edge, he says, is the fact that there are too many mixed blends of honey on the market. 'My rules are too strict for a lot of other keepers. I think other keepers compromise their standards too much.

'To be good, honey has to have a good flavour. It's got to be smooth in your mouth like a good port wine,' he explains. 'I think we undersell too much, even though we're one of the top honey producers in the world. But I think this is the case with all Australian products.'

Although his business is secure, Ian is still concerned about environmental damage and the long-term effects on the beekeeping industry. 'Honey is perhaps not as good quality now as it used to be because of the environment. All these problems have been caused by man. Chemical spraying has had a bad effect. We have 1900 hives at the moment. We used to only need 1110 hives to produce the same amount of honey. We're losing a lot of the reeds and willows, which are a source of high protein, and if you haven't got high protein

in the pollen, the bees don't breed as well, and they go down to diseases.'

Ian has lost count of the number of times he's been stung, but these days it's a rare occurrence. 'A good man can take 100 stings a day,' he smiles, 'but I don't get many now because they reckon I'm too old and don't move fast enough.'

Ian has three sons — Ewan, Neal and Ken — who all work in the business. He plans to hand it over to them once he retires, although he's not quite sure when that will be. He still lives across the road from the honey factory, and has no intention of leaving Mole Creek. 'Being in the one place your whole life is alright,' he smiles. 'It's peaceful. You're not rushing. When I go to bed of a night, I go to sleep. I'm lucky. Why worry about things?'

PULLICAN

Parachilna, South Australia

Born: Adelaide, South Australia, 1957

The Prairie Hotel is located on a dusty plain with the Flinders Ranges as its stunning backdrop. The population of Parachilna is five. Driving towards it, you could easily assume there wouldn't be much more available at this pub than a cold beer, a meat pie and a dowdy old room. Jane Fargher, the Prairie Hotel's publican, will prove your assumptions wildly wrong.

Jane is in the pub's kitchen, preparing the 'feral mixed grill', which includes kangaroo chop, emu sausage, camel steak, wallaby shaslick, bacon and egg, with a bush tomato relish and salad. For the vegetarian diner, there's a spinach, feta and roasted pumpkin triangle with salad;

or for the pie lover, there's a choice of roo and red wine, goat and rosemary, or emu, bacon and mushroom.

'This menu evolved — when we first started we had more traditional homestyle pub food,' Jane explains. 'Then we added kangaroo to the menu and we also made sure there were vegetarian options. We were looking to potential visitors rather than local tastes. The locals know they can come here and ask for anything, and we're happy to accommodate any tastes. The roo was a locally harvested product so we started with it. It was popular and it made us realise that Australian native food wasn't readily available, so we just decided to extend the options.'

Jane and her husband Ross, a pastoralist, took sole ownership of the historic hotel in 1994 after seeing the opportunities in it for outback tourism. The Prairie was first licensed in 1876 and the front of the hotel completed in 1907. 'Ross and I had always looked at what great potential it had as a local hotel. The previous people had always leased it, with difficulty, and there had been a lot of hardship. I just don't think businesses like this are ideal for couples who live and work together — it's a very hard life.

'It was very run down at first. We spent a lot of money which the casual observer wouldn't have noticed, like on electrical wiring and plumbing.

'Then slowly we improved the quality of food and service. We struggled as a one-star establishment with six bedrooms, then we built up an average occupancy of sixty-five per cent with our food reputation, which was quite high for this area, and that prompted us to want to upgrade the facilities. On the rare occasions it rained, the roof leaked and we had to put buckets everywhere!'

The end result was the addition of several rooms, ensuite bathrooms and a conference facility, which were completed in 1997. The following year, the hotel received five different awards — three for tourism, one for best country restaurant and one for architecture. 'We had a lot of problems getting finance because I don't

think a lot of people believed in what we were doing. We'd spent in excess of a million dollars and I guess some people haven't got the optimism or the vision for the future,' Jane comments.

When she married Ross in 1984, Jane's own vision for the future certainly didn't involve running a pub, even though she had spent some time working in the hospitality industry.

Jane grew up on a farming property at Coonalpyn, 160 kilometres south-east of Adelaide. After high school, she did a course in dental therapy and got a job with the health commission. She also worked part-time in hotels, which prompted her to do a hotel management course. This only lasted six months, however, because she got married and went to live on the 570-square-kilometre Nilpena station. Jane met Ross through her sister Di, who is married to Ross's brother Ian. The Fargher brothers are third-generation pastoralists.

'I really liked outdoor work, so I just helped Ross on the station. Ross bought me a motorbike and I was his right-hand man. We were predominantly sheep then, but since the wool industry decline we have changed over to cattle. We didn't employ anyone else, except casually.

'I'd always enjoyed dabbling in a few things and during that time I registered a business name, Far North Bush Clothing, and started selling RM Williams clothes. Then we had the children and I branched into children's clothing.'

Jane has two sons, Lachlan, born in 1986 and Edward, born in 1988.

She travels 220 kilometres a day to get Edward to school in Leigh Creek. Out here, car pooling isn't an option. Lachlan started boarding school in Adelaide in 1999. 'Most people here have their kids on School of the Air, but I guess we believe strongly in the socialisation of schooling, so we put up with the driving. I try to work my hours around school, because Edward gets lonely on his own,' she says.

'The boys love the station life, but we're not encouraging them to go back on the land at the moment. Life on the land without diversification is a pretty humble existence, and I think there are better opportunities for them out there. Without us having diversified, we would have had a pretty tough time on the land.'

Jane admits there have been times when her sons have resented the imposition of the hotel on family life, but by the same token they have met a lot of interesting people, including some from the film and music industry, who have either dined or stayed at the Prairie.

Some of Jane Campion's film *Holy Smoke*, starring Kate Winslet and Harvey Keitel, was filmed there, and Jane often caters for film and advertising crews doing outback shoots. She has also catered for some major music events in Parachilna, including Opera in the Outback. 'It's important to be flexible to cater for these people. They really enjoy the timeless feeling of the landscape here and I don't think you need to be imposing city rules on food times, so we're quite happy to cater for people as they arrive, like cooking hamburgers for breakfast.'

Food has become an important part of tourism, Jane believes. 'I think city people are pleased to come somewhere where they know there's quality of food, a fresh salad, a cappuccino ... just really simple things that aren't difficult to do. It's a really simple formula.'

With standards of outback hospitality lifting, the challenge for Jane and Ross is to be competitive and maintain their leading edge. 'I think we're in a really good position for outback travel and we really see the Australian outback as being such a great asset. We're in a fine position for potential tourism growth. I think what we've proven is that four-wheel drive people aren't just looking for camping and the roughing it experience, because we've got the provision of better quality services here. I think it's opening the outback to higher yield tourism.'

For Jane, the apparent isolation of the pub is just that: apparent. There isn't anything Jane doesn't like about living or working here. 'It always amuses me that people come in and say: "How can you live here, it must be so lonely." It's not! We don't have a lot of close friends, but we have a lot of social interaction. Because it's not a working-class hotel, most of the people who come in are very casual and carefree. I love my workplace, and I don't have many days when I leave here feeling frustrated. There's nothing predictable in our lifestyle.'

DOCTOR AND HOTEL MANAGER

Port Augusta, South Australia

Born: Okara, India (now in Pakistan), 1942

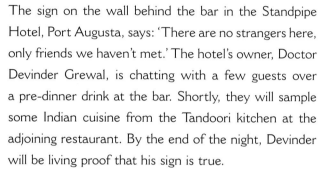

The sign on the wall behind the bar in the Standpipe Hotel, Port Augusta, says: 'There are no strangers here, only friends we haven't met.' The hotel's owner, Doctor Devinder Grewal, is chatting with a few guests over a pre-dinner drink at the bar. Shortly, they will sample some Indian cuisine from the Tandoori kitchen at the adjoining restaurant. By the end of the night, Devinder will be living proof that his sign is true.

Devinder is the maître d' here almost every evening, ensuring the guests at his family-owned, family-managed hotel are comfortable. During the day, he works as a general practitioner in a surgery just down the road from the hotel. 'It's not a strange combination of professions at all — you're always in contact with people and they're both service industries,' Devinder explains of his two seemingly incongruous careers.

A third-generation doctor, Devinder was schooled in both India and Singapore, then returned to India to train in the city of Amritsar, the mecca for Sikhs. With race riots occurring in Penang and Malaysia, Devinder decided he wanted to get away and come to Australia.

'With the White Australia policy going on, I was told I couldn't come into Australia unless I had highly specialised skills, which is why I went to Manchester to study microbiology. I thought if somebody wasn't happy with my black hands delivering their white baby, I could at least handle bacteria,' he says, matter-of-factly.

'I had met a lot of Australians at the Butterworth

base, which is when I decided on Australia. I thought it was the best country to come to. I wanted to bring my children up here, even though I didn't have any kids at that time.'

In 1972, Devinder landed a position as a lecturer in Adelaide but this only lasted seven weeks, until he snatched a GP's vacancy in the town of Quorn, fifty kilometres north-east of Port Augusta.

'In Quorn, I liked the people in particular,' he recalls. 'They were so open and welcoming. They took time to talk to each other and spend time that people don't seem to have in the cities. 'I've never felt not welcome here. I've been one of the lucky people who's had a really good relationship with everyone I've met. I've never felt discriminated against. Funny thing is, I've felt people wanted to find out a bit more about me because they thought I was different.'

Devinder spent ten years in Quorn. When he and his wife Surinder moved to Port Augusta in 1983, they decided to purchase the 100-year-old Standpipe Hotel as a place to live and as a future source of income. It had fifteen rooms and a small restaurant at the time of the purchase, so eventually Devinder added seventy-two rooms and expanded the restaurant to seat two hundred.

'My elder brother told me when I left India to become an employer rather than an employee. Our plan was to diversify, to create an income for our children so that rather than looking for jobs, we were creating jobs,' Devinder explains.

He introduced Indian food to the restaurant one night a week, but it became so popular that in 1995 he changed to serving Indian food throughout the week, and now employs three chefs. Port Augusta is the crossroads for those heading north towards

Devinder and his son, Depinder

the Northern Territory, or heading west across the Nullarbor. Besides the passing motorists on holiday, corporate clients account for much of the hotel's occupancy.

Devinder says he rarely advertises and relies mainly on word of mouth for the hotel business. He gives full credit to his wife, children and three brothers, who all help to manage the hotel. One brother runs a hotel on the other side of town and another brother, who recently arrived from Kuala Lumpur, will soon run a hotel in Whyalla. His youngest son, Depinder, has just completed a degree in hotel management and marketing. 'We have just bought another hotel in the Clare Valley so we'll have a chain of hotels which we'll probably call the Standpipe Group,' Devinder explains.

As a GP, Devinder's role has changed considerably in the past twenty years. The days of the GP handling every procedure are long gone. 'The difference between a GP in the seventies and one in the nineties is that in the seventies, I did half the deliveries in the town each year, 300 anaesthetics and 150 surgical procedures. I don't do any of this stuff now. Now, I see the GP as a friend, a confidante, an adviser, and a source of referrals.'

Devinder is occasionally called out by the Royal Flying Doctor Service and also spends one day a week with the Aboriginal Health Service, an experience he says has been both revealing and rewarding. 'It's depressing in that we haven't made progress in leaps and bounds, but it's gratifying to know there is a slow and steady measurable improvement occurring by the dedicated people working there,' he says.

While he believes the Australian healthcare system is one of the best, he is concerned that the gulf between rich and poor is widening. 'The thing disappearing here is the large middle class. There are more and more people who can't afford private health insurance. If you can afford it, then there are no waiting lists.'

Fortunate enough to consider himself one of the 'haves' rather than the 'have nots', Devinder says he has very little stress in his life. 'Stress is the mismatch of our expectations and the ability of our environment to deliver. So if the environment can deliver every darn thing you and I expect, then there's no stress. Since it can't deliver everything, then you have to alter your expectations.'

A practising Sikh, Devinder believes he has been successful because he loves what he does and sets goals.

'I love my profession. I'm very lucky to have something I think is noble and to improve some illness, or some unhappiness, or pain. One of the founding members of a pharmaceutical company in the 1950s said: "We have to concentrate more on people and less on profit." Rather than worrying about dollars and cents, if you look at every person you meet as a potential salesperson for you, then you can't go wrong. It's the type of people you meet and the memories you have that are more important anyhow.'

MOTHER AND CANCER SUFFERER

Adelaide, South Australia

Born: Adelaide, South Australia, 1965

Laureen and Byron Ford, and their four-year-old grand-daughter Emily, have just returned from a shopping trip to the Adelaide city markets. They are unpacking bags of organic fruit and vegetables for their 34-year-old daughter Julia, who is sitting at the kitchen table, leafing through a healing cancer cookbook.

A roster for Julia's family is taped to the kitchen wall. This evening, Julia's brother Patrick will come and cook dinner; tomorrow, her sister Carolyn will take her daughter Emily to kindergarten; the day after that, her other sister Mary will take her to the doctor and cook her meals; next week, Laureen and Byron will go shopping again.

One month ago, a few days before Emily's fourth birthday, Julia was diagnosed with secondary cancer. Her family are now giving her round-the-clock support, an absolute necessity while she undergoes chemotherapy and an unrelenting series of hospital visits.

Strangely, it was Julia's illness that brought her back home to her family in Adelaide after a long stint away. The youngest of five children, she grew up in the northern suburb of Elizabeth Grove. She worked at the General Motors Holden plant for three years, then for Hanimex as a photographic printer. At twenty-one she married Rick, a man she had met at the GMH plant. They both yearned to do a long caravan trip around Australia, so they saved for four years, and set off in 1990. They worked as they travelled, spending four-and-a-half years away, two of those years on Queensland's Gold Coast.

In 1994 they reached Perth and decided to settle there. Julia found work with a photo company, Rick at a steel plant. They bought a block of land intending to build a house, and Julia soon got pregnant. She had wanted a child for a long time, but Rick didn't feel the same way. Their relationship deteriorated after Emily's birth, and they broke up six months later. 'One night he just said to me, "I don't feel the same about you as I did." I was totally devastated and cried for a few nights,' Julia recalls.

Shattered by the split, Julia went home to Adelaide for four months, but returned to Perth to try and start her life over, this time as a single mother. She found it difficult. 'It wasn't really a bad life, it was good, because it was just Emily and me. But I think I missed out on a lot because she was in daycare. I missed out on bringing her up, and doing all those wonderful things with her. I was resentful towards Rick for that fact.'

In September 1997, eighteen months after returning to Perth, Julia was diagnosed with bowel cancer. In the space of two weeks, she packed up everything and returned to live with her sister Carolyn in Adelaide.

Left to right: Byron, Carolyn, Emily, Julia and Laureen

She had major surgery, followed by a five-month course of chemotherapy. During this time, Emily lived with Julia's parents.

As she began to recuperate from the chemotherapy, Julia felt prompted to make some changes in her life. 'I filed for divorce and cleared that up. It made me want to go out and grasp at things now, instead of doing them later. I should have made more changes then. I was going to do meditation and had looked into changing my diet, but I didn't stick to any of it the first time. The thing I didn't like about having treatment is that I didn't like me as a person, because I didn't have patience for Emily like I used to, so every little thing she did, I couldn't handle.'

As Julia recovered, however, she was able to spend more time with Emily because she wasn't working. Her health continued to improve and she had blood tests every three months, so she was completely unprepared for the second diagnosis in April 1999. 'I had this pain under my ribs and the GP told me it was from straining my muscles at golf.' But after continued pain and some more tests, Julia learned the cancer had spread to her liver and one lung. She was told chemotherapy would only prolong her life, and that no treatment would eliminate the cancer.

'I didn't expect the news to be bad. I went in on my own and he told me to go and get Mary and then he told us it wasn't good news. We both started crying. I was so shocked. He was pretty cold-hearted, he just sat behind his table. I asked why a scan wasn't done a year ago, and he said it wouldn't have mattered if a scan had been done three months ago, that it wouldn't have shown up then. A liver transplant wasn't feasible, because the cancer is floating around in my body.

'We left the room and I was just a total f***ing mess, you know. I had to walk out into a waiting room full of people. I hit this wall a couple of times and this nurse came out and asked me if I was alright. She went and got someone for me and they put me in another room.

'I was pretty numb. I cried quite a lot at first. I wasn't eating anything. It was just like a dream, it wasn't happening to me.' Julia found some immediate support with a counselling session at the Cancer Council, and later did a Coping with Cancer course, which she found helpful.

As she underwent chemotherapy and became less capable, her family rallied around her with physical, practical and emotional support. Believing in the potential to heal herself, Julia began meditating, and eating organic foods. 'It's not so much that I'm disillusioned with doctors, I just think this is the only way I'm going to be able to heal myself. The doctors don't give me much help anyway. You hear so many different stories of people who've had three weeks to live, and twenty or thirty years down the track they're still with us, and they did it with their minds,' she says passionately. 'I'm learning about the body and what the mind can do, that it's so powerful. The places I can take my body to is amazing. I can go into this room filled with bright light and your body feels warm and yet you're just listening to a tape.'

Naturally, Emily has struggled to understand her mother's illness. 'I've told her I'm sick and I have to work on myself to get me better, which involves a lot of time I can't spend with her. She was really quite angry the first time she stayed with Mum and Dad. She told them, "I don't like you, I just want it to be me and my mum." I asked her why she was so angry. I said, "Is it because you want to make your mummy well?" And she said, "Yes I do." I think to go through this at such a young age must be so hard for her,' Julia says, her eyes filling with tears.

It is her daughter, though, who sustains Julia's spirit from day to day. 'Emily is the thing that makes me stay positive because I'm going to be the one bringing her up. No-one else is, because they wouldn't be able to bring her up in the way I can bring her up, because I'm a wonderful person and I want her to have my sick and sorry sense of humour,' she laughs her deep chesty laugh, 'and she can't have that if I'm not around. I just want so many things for her, so I'm going to be here to see them through. I'm staying focused on my life. The fact that someone is trying to take my life away from me early — I'm not happy with that. It's not going to happen.'

Postscript

Despite her positive spirit and brave fight, Julia lost her battle with cancer six months after the second diagnosis, and passed away in the Mary Potter Hospice, Adelaide, at 6.40 am on 21 October 1999.

In the eulogy, Julia was described as a 'very friendly, open person, courageous with great determination. She worried about the people who were caring for her, how they were coping and she was just so incredibly accepting of her situation, that she taught us all many things.'

Emily now lives with Julia's sister, Carolyn, and her family.

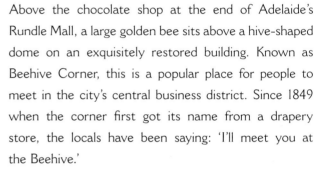

HERITAGE OFFICER
Adelaide, South Australia
Born: North Adelaide, South Australia, 1954

Paul Stark

Above the chocolate shop at the end of Adelaide's Rundle Mall, a large golden bee sits above a hive-shaped dome on an exquisitely restored building. Known as Beehive Corner, this is a popular place for people to meet in the city's central business district. Since 1849 when the corner first got its name from a drapery store, the locals have been saying: 'I'll meet you at the Beehive.'

Paul Stark, a heritage officer with the Adelaide City Council, glances up with a well-earned sense of satisfaction every time he walks past this heritage building. Walk around town with him, and he'll proudly show you a few more historic buildings with which he shares a close connection. Adelaide's architecture is the distinctive feature, the showpiece, of the city. Adelaide City Council is recognised nationally for its heritage conservation program, and tourist exit surveys have continually shown that its architecture is noticed.

Paul has worked for the Council since 1981. He studied architecture at the University of Adelaide, specialising in conservation after a trip to Europe at the end of first year, which opened his eyes to the historical significance of buildings. 'I saw a house in Lincoln which is 900 years old and still in use, and cathedrals which date from the ninth century. It's the evidence of history over 2000 years, whereas European settlement here has a time scale of 150 or 200 years. These were things that impressed a rather impressionable youth in Europe for the first time, so it was pivotal in skewing my career moves.'

Paul was first employed by the National Trust. One of his early projects was to carry out regional surveys and update the documentation on heritage properties. 'I had to cast my net wide in looking for buildings that had been missed in previous heritage surveys, from Gawler to the Upper Murray through the Adelaide Hills up to Clare. It was a wonderful experience. It was exciting having to photograph these buildings for the records.

'The National Trust had a charter of recording and working towards the retention of buildings. It was the only organisation that kept a register of important buildings. The 1978 *South Australian Heritage Act*, which established a register of heritage items, took on much of this material that had been built up by the National Trust.'

In 1981 Paul was part of a team commissioned to do a heritage study for the Adelaide City Council. This study resulted in the first local heritage register for the city. 'In establishing this register, the council wanted to make sure that when properties were listed, there was a management program to assist the owners in looking after these buildings because, in quite an enlightened way, they realised that much of the city's heritage was in private ownership,' Paul explains.

In 1987 Paul went to York, England, to do a Master's degree in Conservation Studies, returning to work for the Council again in 1988. His present role is to assist the management of change to any heritage-listed buildings. In 1999 there were 1,700 heritage-listed properties in Adelaide. The Council assists private owners to undertake about 150 conservation projects a year, depending on demand and the budget.

'These buildings, even though they are heritage listed, are not museum pieces,' says Paul. 'They still have to work for the private owner and be viable, or liveable. What we encourage is a pretty pragmatic reconciliation of cultural qualities, and practical and economic needs.'

The shining example of this is the restoration of the Beehive Corner, a project fully financed by the Council at a cost of $680,000, in a combination of loans and grants to the owners. The building, occupied by multiple owners, required extensive and detailed restoration work to its facade, which had gone through numerous changes since being built in 1896.

'Council offered to sponsor a conservation plan which identified the needs of the building and allowed a better understanding of the cultural qualities of it. Some gables had been removed, some were covered; some parts were covered in metal siding. The original bee had either been taken off or lost after the 1954 earthquake. It needed a lot of work. We knew once this building was done, it would be an example of what could be achieved.'

The Beehive project was completed in 1998. Other large heritage restoration projects with which Paul has been associated include the Luther Seminary, the Wests Coffee Palace and the Botanic Chambers.

In terms of putting conservation and planning skills into practice, Australia is among the best in the world, and is now exporting these heritage skills to the Asia-Pacific region.

'The reason we're so good at it,' says Paul, 'may have something to do with the fact that we're a very energetic country and we like to do things well.' Another reason is the 1976 code of practice known as the Burra Charter. 'In Europe, there was the Venice Charter, which set the standards and protocols in looking after old fabric, be it a building or a road, or whatever,' he explains. 'We wanted to particularise this charter to Australia's needs. It was the first time that another country, other than some in the old world, had done it. Here was a country in the new world doing it. This charter put the conservation industry here in very good standing.'

What makes preserving our heritage so important, Paul believes, is the contribution it makes to our history and sense of place.

'People have a collective memory about the Beehive Corner. Even when I met girlfriends in town, you'd meet at the Beehive. It's part of that social fabric. Groupings of buildings can be considered social history on a grand scale. In North Adelaide, you have an assemblage of grand houses on boulevards, then around the corner you have smaller houses, representing those of more modest means. They give you a historical understanding of the genesis of the city. Many owners get a lot of pride from owning part of the city's heritage, and that's a terrific attitude.

'More globally, it's that sense of difference which distinguishes Adelaide from Melbourne and other cities. We don't have Sydney Harbour, we don't have the Swan River, but the environmental and lifestyle qualities of Adelaide and its distinctive character are contributed to considerably by its buildings.'

Living in Adelaide is a constant delight for Paul. 'The work, the people, the opportunities that I have to work on such buildings …' he pauses thoughtfully, adding: 'Our oldest buildings may date back only 160 years but this is our heritage. The Beehive Corner is our Windsor castle.'

FACTORY WORKER
Berri, South Australia
Born: Barmera, South Australia, 1945

Meredith Draper

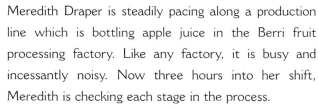

Meredith Draper is steadily pacing along a production line which is bottling apple juice in the Berri fruit processing factory. Like any factory, it is busy and incessantly noisy. Now three hours into her shift, Meredith is checking each stage in the process.

Located in a rich citrus-growing area, this factory is one of eleven operated by Berri Limited, the largest fruit processor in Australia. The company began in the 1940s when a number of co-operatives in the South Australian Riverland district joined together to supply fruit juice to the armed forces. It now packages almost fifty per cent of all fruit juice beverages sold in Australia, and employs 1,400 people nationally. Meredith, who grew up in the small town of Barmera about twenty kilometres away, is one of about 200 employees in the factory at Berri.

'I had a sheltered life, really, until I was seventeen and went to Burra (140 kilometres north of Barmera) to do nursing. I studied for three years but I didn't graduate. I did two years in a country hospital, then I was supposed to go to the city and I went to Adelaide, but I got homesick so I left and came home. I didn't give myself a good enough chance at it, I can see that looking back now. I think the training was very good because in the country you had a go at everything. We had births, deaths, accidents — everything.'

Meredith met a shearer in Burra and married him soon after returning to Barmera. They had three children in the space of three years. 'When I gave up the nursing

to get married, the nurses' board sent me papers to become an enrolled nurse and at the time, I thought: "I won't have to work." So I didn't even do that, which was a bit silly.'

Meredith's father-in-law was a shearing contractor so she found work cooking for the shearers, travelling with her husband from job to job. 'Financially, we battled. The shearers got good money, but in between each shed they had living and travelling expenses. They might work a month in one shed and by the time they travelled they'd miss a week somewhere, so the money was irregular. We travelled around with two young kids, but by the time I was pregnant a third time, I said: "Well I'm not going to drag three children around in a caravan." So then I came back to Barmera.'

In 1971, by the time her eldest child was seven, Meredith and her husband separated. 'We just drifted apart. We didn't argue or anything,' she recalls. Although her husband was paying maintenance, it wasn't enough to live on, so Meredith found work picking wine and table grapes.

'It was pretty daunting, having to find work on my own. When I went grape picking, I took the kids out on the block with me and they would play under the vines with other kids. I did that for ten years and I loved it. We'd have a ball because it was the same group of people each year. I made good friends.'

In 1973 Meredith met her current husband, Denis, a mechanical engineer. He had returned to live with his parents after being divorced, and lived in the house next door. They married in 1981. That same year, Meredith found work at the Berri factory.

'My first job was working on the two-litre pasteurised juice line. They used to put the little foil shrinkie on the

bottle tops. We put them on by hand, then they went through the heat tunnel to be sealed. Then I went to the blow moulding section and stayed there for nine years. It was repetitious, the work, but we were like a family with the same crew each day, so you became bonded. Unless there was a breakdown, you were working flat chat for the eight hours and it went quick.'

Meredith works four days a week, from 5.30 am to 4.30 pm. She is now a 'leading hand' on the cordial line. 'Which means,' she laughs, 'I get all the kicks in the bum. I relieve our people on their breaks, make sure the quality is there, and oversee everything to keep things moving. If you can't fix a problem, then you get someone who can. I walk 100 yards from one end of the line to the other. I must walk miles every day. Sometimes my legs and feet ache, but I am tough and it's good because it keeps me fit.'

Meredith enjoys going to work, admitting she gets restless after a week of holiday, and says she feels a sense of achievement about what she does. 'I feel proud when I go into shops and see our product there. When I go shopping, I take note of the products and compare other brand names and look at their presentation.'

Meredith and Denis do two trips each year in their caravan — one to the beach in Adelaide, and the other to the Barmera Caravan Park, which is only ten minutes drive from their home. 'We go after Christmas and take our bikes and speedboat. Sometimes we take our ten-year-old grandson with us. I come home to sleep and to feed the dog. It's like we're away but we're not away. Sometimes I have to work during this time.

'I see myself as a battler and we're still battlin'. We don't go without but we're modest. We have three cars but they're all old. Our TV is old as the hills and when it goes we might buy one second hand. We nearly own the house — it'll be two more years before we own it. I don't want for anything — I have a roof over my head and a car to get me to work. But when I retire I'd like to have the finances to do things like to go to Adelaide for a week to see the footy or whatever.'

OPAL MINER
Coober Pedy, South Australia
Born: Berri, South Australia, 1950

The white minibus is making its way around the treeless brown dirt streets of Coober Pedy. Di Enders, or 'Lady Di' as she likes to be known, is at the wheel, giving the personal, cheerful spiel she gives at the start of every tour.

'I'll guarantee you that by the time you've finished my tour, you'll have changed your attitude about Coober Pedy. Whether you end up loving it or hating it, at the very least you'll remember it,' she tells the group of tourists on board. 'People who come back here for a second look will say the place hasn't changed, and when I ask them why they've come back, they'll say because they couldn't believe it the first time!'

Located 600 kilometres north of Adelaide and 600 kilometres south of Alice Springs, Coober Pedy is, arguably, a town in the middle of nowhere. Its name, which is Aboriginal, means 'white man in hole', a reference to the opal miners who have dug hundreds of holes in search of, as Di calls them, 'the queen of the gems'.

Di is an opal miner, but like so many of the miners in Coober Pedy, a regular job is a financial necessity. She works at the Oasis Caravan Park, which her parents have owned since 1990, and runs the bus tours from there.

She had lived in suburban Adelaide and worked as a postal services officer for eighteen years when, in 1994, her twenty-seven year marriage came to an end. She went to Coober Pedy for eight weeks to run the caravan park with her sister, so her parents could have a holiday. It was her first visit to the town and she fell in love with it immediately. 'I was totally in awe of it — the difference, the uniqueness, the dirt,' Di explains. 'Here, there is dirt and more dirt.'

In the caravan park, Di met Wolfgang, a German engineer who 'chucked it all in', according to Di, to dig for opal after seeing a television show on Coober Pedy. 'I convinced him what he needed more than opal was me, so I married him,' she laughs.

Di started mining with Wolfgang in 1995, learning the ropes the hard way. 'The first time down the ladder, I froze halfway down because I got claustrophobic. It took me two hours to climb down seventy-five foot of ladder. My legs wouldn't keep still. I got down by sheer damn determination. Then I went into a corner and composed myself and I've never looked back.'

Coober Pedy's opal fields stretch for just under 5000 square kilometres. In the 1970s and 1980s, there were up to 2000 miners here; in 1999, there were only 150. 'There's no new blood coming in. The trouble is, we haven't had a new opal field found here for twelve years, and nobody can afford to go prospecting anymore.'

Like most of the miners, Di pegs old mine claims and reworks them because opal mining is a very costly

mining is an obsession, an addiction, and if you didn't have that you could never continue here,' she says in the next breath.

'When I go out noodling [searching through the scrap heaps] on tours — I can't help myself, I love it — I find small bits and I get totally rapt. I have it in my veins. I know I'm going to find opal, there's no doubt about it. People are still finding opal here all the time. We're just one of the unlucky ones, that's all. I know out there there's a bit of opal with Lady Di on it, the only trouble is, I'm having trouble finding it.'

They call opal miners the 'million dollar gamblers', a title Di resents. 'I've worked my butt off. It's a gamble in the respect that I don't know if it's going to pay me back, but it doesn't matter because it's an experience.'

Di is building a 'dugout' — an underground home — which will make the six months of high temperatures more bearable. The intense heat is really the only aspect of life here that she does not handle well.

If the town is labelled as a place for escapists, then so be it, says Di. 'There's no stress, no pollution, you can do your own thing. You don't have to put on this facade. Here, I can be myself, do what I like and if that means escape — well, being bottled up in a city isn't much good.

'I would hate to go back into suburbia again. When I was there I felt cornered, as if there was no escape.'

When the isolation and insulation of Coober Pedy closes in on Di, she gets in her car and goes for a drive. A 450-kilometre drive.

'As soon as you get in the car and leave, you think: "Yes!" But when you get to Port Augusta and get to that first traffic light, you want to turn back. Then you go into a shopping centre and see all the beautiful fresh fruit and vegies — but then you see all the people, and cars, and you can't stand it. I can't stand the hustle and bustle.'

business. 'All out, we've gone through — oh, say tens of thousands of dollars. We've got all our machinery because we've bought piles of junk that nobody else wanted, and Wolfgang has rebuilt it. It's not a viable business. It's ninety per cent luck and 110 per cent damn hard work.'

Di has set herself a goal of ten years to find opal but five years in, she hasn't found much. 'Wolfgang had high hopes but I didn't. I knew it wasn't going to be easy. We found a few stones at first, we found the one in my pendant and my ring, and thought it was going to be okay, but for the last three-and-a-half years all we have found is $900 worth.

'The enthusiasm is gone, the drive is gone, and you just drag your feet from day to day,' she sighs. 'But opal

BREWER
Adelaide, South Australia
Born: Adelaide, South Australia, 1932

'Good morning, Mr Bill,' the secretary greets Bill Cooper as he walks into the administration office upstairs from the brewery. Bill smiles back warmly. There are four other Mr Coopers who work for this family-run company, so in the interests of good communication, no-one is called Mr Cooper.

Coopers Brewery sits in the leafy Adelaide suburb of Norwood. The company was founded by Bill's great-grandfather, Thomas Cooper, in 1862 and the production house, where Bill now works, was built in 1881. Thomas Cooper brewed the original Sparkling Ale as a tonic for his ill wife Anne, then began selling it directly to friends and neighbours. When he died in 1897, he left the business to his four sons.

Bill spent the first nineteen years of his life in the house next door to the Norwood brewery. 'My brother Robert and I were crawling all over this place from the very early years. It was wartime and we used to hitch a ride to school on the horse-drawn brewery wagons. As a kid, the most fascinating side of it was to take a sickie, then miraculously recover at 10 am and go and watch the blacksmith making horseshoes. I could still watch a fella do that, I think. It's an art.'

When Bill finished high school, he won a scholarship to Adelaide University and studied science, but considered it dreadful and quit to go jackarooing instead. 'My brother Robert was an engineer and already working for the company so there was no pressure on

me to do the same. In the eighteen months I was jackarooing, I really learnt what hard work was all about. I'm still grateful to that farmer for taking this callow, soft youth and hardening me up!

'Succession is alive and well in this company. You can't come in here with a silver spoon and expect to work for the rest of your life. You have to go out and do something else before you work here.'

Bill spent six years running a sheep and cattle farm at Mt Compass. When his brother Robert was accidentally killed in 1956, his father began putting some pressure on him to join the company. But it wasn't until 1959, when Bill got blood poisoning from a grass seed in his finger and spent six weeks extremely ill in hospital, that he decided to quit farming and return to Adelaide.

'I was very resistant at first, but I could see the logic in it in the end,' he says.

Although Bill's father was a brewer, Bill knew nothing about making beer when he arrived. His cousin Max, however, had been in charge of brewing since 1953 and boasted a science degree in it, so he took Bill under his wing. The traditional recipe, which hasn't changed since 1862, had to stay within the family. 'One of the Cooper family had to physically put the brew in. It was called mashing in the brew. We all took it in turns month by month, and you worked your life around this roster. We did one brew a day in those days. Now, we do seven brews a day, seven days a week.'

The traditional red-label, heavy-sediment beer, Coopers Ale, used to be brewed in wooden vats, piped

off and conditioned in 500-litre wooden casks. 'All those barrels had to be rolled upstairs, then rinsed out with soda ash, then sterilised, then slipped down into the cellar again. It involved an enormous amount of work. We had seventeen men doing that job to produce four or five brews a week. You couldn't do this now,' says Bill. 'We worked for four years to switch to stainless-steel kegs, but still retain the same characteristics of our beer. We have a whole cupboard of every record of every brew we've made. Sometimes you can get slight variations in flavour, but it's one of the characteristics of our ale because each brew is an individual one.'

Bill points out that the Australian beer market was very insular in the 1960s and 1970s. 'You couldn't buy Tooheys beer in Brisbane, for instance. You could always buy Carlton beer in Queensland as they owned breweries in that state, but it would be hard to find it in New South Wales, for example. It was state bound. We tried very hard — with a modicum of success — to sell interstate. I used to get criticism about trying to sell interstate. It sounds quaint now, doesn't it?' he laughs.

Stout, which was supplied to the armed forces during World War II and often prescribed for medicinal purposes, was the bestselling product when Bill first joined the company. The other major product was the Sparkling Ale, the cloudy-looking beer which remains one of Coopers' trademarks. 'The other brewery was promoting "clear sparkling beer", which was a shot at us, and our ale dropped from favour,' Bill explains. 'Then all of a sudden in the early 1970s, the ale took off in spectacular fashion, despite a total lack of advertising. We learned it was young people buying it and the basic reason was because they'd discovered it and it wasn't the beer that Dad drank.'

When Bill's father retired in 1969, Bill became company secretary and a director. He took over as managing director in 1977. The four other 'Mr Coopers' presently with the company are: Maxwell, the chairman; Glenn, marketing director; Dr Timothy,

operations director; and James, a member of the board, along with Glenn and Timothy.

Coopers is the only family-owned brewery in Australia. It has an annual turnover of $85 million and it produces 1.1 million hectalitres of beer, home brew and malt extract annually. The home brew market, which accounts for thirty per cent of Coopers' sales, is a tale of personal triumph for Bill. 'We were keeping wort sterile in a plastic bag and we found we could keep it sterile for a year. It was so simple, because you just took the top out of the bag, put the yeast in and put a couple of holes in to let it breathe, then bottled it five days later. We realised we could sell it to home brewers and that's how we went into home brew. When I told the Associated Brewers of Australia about it, they told me it was something I shouldn't do. We said, "We think it will stimulate an interest in beer." One of the brewers sought to expel us for making the home brew, but that didn't eventuate. Now we're the largest producer of canned home brew in the world. We have eighty per cent of Sweden's market, sixty per cent of the Finnish, and we're quite substantial in Britain. The company has survived very well and no doubt there'll be more ups and downs, but as long as you have the ability to adapt you'll survive,' says Bill.

Three of Bill's four children have worked for the company. 'I discouraged them all first and told them to go out and get experience,' he explains. His daughter Melanie, an accountant, was assistant financial controller and company secretary for a period, but had to move to Brisbane. 'Up until she came, it was Cooper and Sons, so we had to change the name,' laughs Bill. Both his sons are helping keep up the family tradition. Matthew works in the distribution centre at Regency Park. Timothy, who did degrees in medicine and business first, eventually completed a degree in brewing in the UK, then returned to work in production. 'Tim said to me: "Dad, I've seen a lot of unhappy doctors, but I've never seen an unhappy brewer,"' Bill says with a broad, knowing smile.

CLOTHING DESIGNER
Port Lincoln, South Australia
Born: Adelaide, South Australia, 1969

It is the colours that confront you when you walk into Sue Catt-Green's aptly named clothing store — *Colors* — in Port Lincoln. Just behind the racks of handmade clothes, Sue is sitting at a sewing machine in her workshop, putting together another unique garment. She is surrounded by colour. There are handpainted silk shirts, loud cocktail dresses, bright trousers and vivid skirts, each item designed and constructed by Sue.

Sue acknowledges her shop seems out of place in this tuna fishing town. In Melbourne, Byron Bay or Brisbane it would seem quite ordinary, but in Port Lincoln the locals think it kind of unusual.

'My mother is a dressmaker and has a frock shop in town,' Sue explains, 'and someone said to her the other day: "Sue has such lovely stuff, but I wouldn't ever wear it."

'Sometimes I think I'm banging my head against a brick wall trying to sell these clothes to people here, but I am finding that tourists are buying them. Some people come in and say it's over the top with all the colour. I'm finding there's not too many people in Port Lincoln who want different things.'

After growing up in Port Lincoln, Sue moved to Adelaide at the age of seventeen to study fashion design. Her mother's influence had instilled the desire for a career in fashion from an early age.

Sue set up her own dressmaking business from her Adelaide home as soon as she graduated, relying

STEVE GREEN
Iron artist
sculptural & functional
at work
made-to-order
Ph/Fax 08 86834530

on word of mouth to bring in customers. 'I decided I didn't want to work for anyone else and I've worked for myself ever since. I was probably a bit naive at the time, but I just did it,' she recalls.

'I did lots of wedding dresses. I also made clothes for people who couldn't find things to fit, or people just wanting something a bit different that they couldn't find in all the other boutiques.'

In 1995 Sue and her husband Steve established their first *Colors* clothing shop in the beachside suburb of Glenelg, but after one year of good trading, high rents forced her to work from home again.

When Sue fell pregnant with her first child Jasper, in 1996, the couple decided to return to Port Lincoln, where they knew they could both count on family support. Sue realised her business potential here would be limited when compared with Adelaide, but she

and Steve wanted to raise their children in a smaller community, with 'country air'.

Despite her certainty with this decision, Sue admits adjusting to life in Port Lincoln again has been difficult.

'It's been hard to settle back down. It's very cliquey. We're having trouble finding new friends here.

'I'm glad I moved away though. You've got to get out of a small town to broaden your mind. So many people here are just stuck because they don't know any different. It's frustrating talking to people who don't know any different.'

For Sue, the ten years away changed her considerably.

'I have a lot more confidence. I'm more opinionated. I'm set in what I believe in, in what I know and what I'm trying to get people to look at in their own lives,' she says thoughtfully.

Sue considers herself a separate entity from the

mainstream fashion industry, and has always resisted becoming a part of it.

'Going mainstream just doesn't appeal to me, because you have to mass produce. You lose creative control of what you're doing. I wouldn't be able to put in individual detail — I couldn't handpaint a silk shirt fifty times, for example.

'I am aware of how the industry works, but I'm not interested in getting an agent and having to make ranges every season because I want to keep it individual and keep pieces as one-offs. I'm not trying to compete anymore.'

Most fashion designers, Sue believes, dictate clothing styles that are unsuitable for a major portion of the population, particularly women.

'I think it's ridiculous when the designers say you should wear this one season and that the other season. At the moment the fashions are just dreadful. If that's what women are supposed to wear, I feel sorry for them. Half the time they don't suit anybody unless they're stick thin and sixteen years old. I believe you should be wearing stuff that suits you, in colours that suit you, and that way you're going to feel better about yourself anyway. I want my pieces to be comfortable, to fit into people's lifestyles without being too constrictive.'

Late in 1999, Sue and Steve finished building a new home on rural land with water views just outside town. Sue's second child, Daisy, was born in February 2000. After living in a flat above her shop for two years, Sue was looking forward to separating her work and home environments, and spending a little more time with her children. Steve, a concreter by trade, has been constructing scupltures from wrought iron in recent years and after one successful joint exhibition with Sue, they plan on doing more.

Sue's designs, it seems, are a reflection of her philosophy on life.

'You have to be true to yourself,' she says, without hesitation. 'And try and be happy as much as possible.'

SURFER

Red Bluff, Western Australia

Born: Sydney, New South Wales, 1970

Taras Mulik

Red Bluff is an isolated stretch of Western Australia's coast with a bushy green headland that overlooks a white sandy beach and a turquoise-blue ocean. To reach it, you drive seventy kilometres along an isolated stretch of sandy road, which can get very boggy, especially after rain. In a two-wheel drive you feel lucky to get through, but when you arrive, you're suprised to see two-wheel drives parked everywhere. The foreshore is dotted with panel vans, tents, station wagons and caravans, all flagged by towels and wetsuits, flapping in the breeze. They belong to the full-time surfers, who spend the winter months here, surfing the world-class waves.

On the southern end of the beach is a cave, a rocky hideaway beneath the headland, which this winter is home to Taras Mulik. 'It's first in, best dressed. I got here in June and there was no-one in the cave, so I jumped in,' he explains, as he buffs his board in front of the cave, repairing a crease.

His friends — Brad, a fisherman, and his girlfriend, Cheryl — are visiting for a few weeks, sitting behind him, reading thick paperbacks in the shade. Taras is waiting for the wind to drop before he goes in for his first surf of the day.

'I first found out about Red Bluff from a good friend of mine who always used to disappear in winter. When I quizzed him, he told me about it, so I thought I'd have a look and I'm glad I did, because that was about nine years ago now. When I came up the first time with a

friend, I hitched here and camped in a little tent. I didn't have much at all. The waves were so good, I stayed for three or four months. I don't think I've missed a winter here since,' he says, smiling at the ocean.

Taras lives for good waves. He spends his winters surfing at Red Bluff and the remainder of the year surfing on the south coast, at Margaret River. If he saves enough money, he tries to have a surfing trip to Indonesia in between. 'I try and stay up here for as long as my money lasts. I wait for it to warm up again down south before I go back. The hardest thing about this place is leaving.'

His life has followed pretty much the same pattern since he was twenty. He got used to travelling as a child because his mother, an art teacher, was 'a bit of a hippie who roamed around a bit'. He spent his early childhood in the northern NSW town of Mullumbimby, came to live in Perth at the age of six, and learned how to surf relatively late, at the age of fifteen.

In the years after high school, Taras worked as a

surfboard repairer and deckhand for an abalone diver. In the summer he usually finds work doing surfboard shaping and repairs. For the remainder of the year, he lives on unemployment benefits, a fact he carries little guilt about. 'Ten per cent of Australia own this country's wealth, so if people paid their taxes right, then the percentage of people on unemployment benefits wouldn't really make a major difference, if the money was shared around evenly. I've done a lot of work and I've paid taxes. When I've earned good coin, a lot of it has gone into tax. You don't get much back. There's no use working for the weekend if you're not enjoying it.'

Taras sleeps in his van and uses the cave for living space. He has a gas fridge and gas cooker in the cave, and lives mostly off the fresh fish he catches every day. He pays $5 a night camping fee.

An average day for Taras goes like this. 'Generally I wake up fairly early, when the morning stars are still in the sky. When I wake up, I look straight out at the ocean from my van. You look out to the point and if there's a decent amount of white water there, you go out surfing. If not, then it's a good time to go fishing. I have a cast of lure, sometimes I catch crabs in the rocks for bait. Then I come back and eat my Weetbix! After a morning surf, I'll often cook fish for lunch. Sometimes I'll catch crayfish or squid — every sort of fish you can imagine. If you need some food, then you'll write a little list and whoever is going into town (Carnarvon) will get it for you. There's no 'have tos' or 'not have tos'. If you run out of milk, it's not a big deal. We all share. In the afternoons I'll surf, or read, or fish later on. At night we sit around the fire and talk about the day's events — the fishing or the surfing — or play the guitar.'

For Taras, surfing is a lifestyle and an addiction. Living at Red Bluff puts him in touch with nature and makes him appreciate simple pleasures. 'It's a big relief when you get here, you feel yourself unwind after the first week and get back to basics. I've always had the philosophy that the more you've got, the more you've got to worry about, whether it be mortgages or power bills, so it makes it heaps easier to live here.

'If you go more than a couple of weeks without a surf, you can really notice your health going downhill. You have more thoughts on your mind. It's like meditation in a way. When you're out there, you're not thinking of any day-to-day stresses. It's sort of like a healing process, I suppose.

'The sea-life is the beauty of being here. You get all sorts of sharks here — mainly reef and bronze whalers. I see them every day. Some guys were hand feeding them with fish scraps the other day. I've seen humpback whales cruise out the back, close enough to see big barnacles growing on their sides. Sometimes they come in and stay with their calves. We get dolphins as well. After a while we take it for granted. I suppose Japanese tourists would pay a lot of good money to come here and see what we get to see.'

Although he doesn't consider himself talented enough to be a professional, Taras says you need to be very confident to surf at the Bluff. 'It's such a fast wave here, it's not a place for beginners. It's a challenging wave, to say the least. I've hit the bottom of the reef a few times, but that's to be expected.'

Taras has made all his best friends in his time at Red Bluff. He sees a big contrast between the type of person living in a small community like his surfing fraternity, and the suburban city dweller. He says he can easily see himself still coming to Red Bluff in his forties and fifties.

'This is my favourite place on the whole earth, just knowing you have so many good friends here, and the cost of living being so minimal. It's good to know you have places like this where you really feel comfortable. This is one of the places I would call home.'

BOOK DESIGNER/ ILLUSTRATOR

Broome, Western Australia

Born: Perth, Western Australia, 1972

A small building in the suburban back streets of Broome is the home of Magabala Books, one of only three Aboriginal publishing houses in the country. Inside, Sam Cook, a young book designer and illustrator, is at her computer, working on the layout of a new title. On her desk is a pottery trophy of a gecko, an award from the National Aboriginal and Islander Day Observance Committee (NAIDOC) for 1999 Youth of the Year. Sam was recognised for her contributions to her local

indigenous community, made mostly through her work.

Sam is the only indigenous designer of Aboriginal books in the country, and is thrilled about the award. 'Being so remote means I never get peer assessment on my work. I just tend to work with my head down without any feedback. So it was really good to win, and quite an honour to have that recognition from the national community.'

Sam's sense of Aboriginal heritage was instilled in her by her mother Phillipa, who was quite politically active during Sam's early years. 'The Aboriginal side of my family is my mother's side. They're the Nyikina people, who were based between Derby and Looma. I was brought up around the tent embassies in Perth with my mum, and she always made sure we came back to visit family here. I've been attending corroborees and gatherings since I was a baby. I remember going out fishing in the communities. There's always been a sense of community and culture in our family, even before I was born.'

Her father, Peter, is a federal politician who divides his time between Canberra and Perth. Sam's parents divorced when she was eight, so she spent most of her childhood in Broome with her mother and three siblings.

'There's never been any sudden realisation of my identity — it's always been there' Sam explains. 'I've been really fortunate in that respect, because for a lot of Aboriginal people, their identity has been taken away from them and they're still trying to find it. I was lucky that my "mimi" — my grandmother's mother — didn't have her children taken away from her, so the family unit stayed together. The close linking of the family has always been there.'

Sam completed high school at Nulungu Catholic College, and then went to Perth where she did a Bachelor of Fine Arts, majoring in computer animation and video production. A six-month trip to Los Angeles in 1992 with her sister opened her eyes to the world. 'We were doing what any wide-eyed twenty-year-olds would do!' she smiles. 'You don't realise how beautiful

Broome is until you leave it and you get caught up in the smog of LA, and the beaches pale in comparison.'

In 1994, she landed a traineeship in book design at Magabala Books. In the five years with the company, she has designed twenty-nine books, and her position has evolved into a highly specialised one. 'It's more than just book design, it's a very specific role in terms of liaison with Aboriginal artists, writers and arts agencies around the country,' she explains.

When a manuscript comes in, the work is read by Magabala's committee, who make recommendations regarding the title, marketing, its significance, and its cultural or community importance. 'Sometimes even if a book isn't highly marketable but it's significant culturally, we still publish it. We have to do a lot of cultural checking with each book to make sure it's accepted, especially in terms of language. Then I

Four generations

start checking on art or photos in terms of their appropriateness. I make contact with artists and get them working on different material.'

For illustrated books, Sam often liaises with community artists, many based in remote locations, guiding them with the kind of artwork most suited to the book. 'I always try and incorporate the essence of the story into the design of the book. I also try and encourage artists to develop their skills. For example, a woman doing a children's book sent in a series of pencil drawings which really lent themselves to collage. She had never done collage before, so I sent her some materials with explanatory notes and she sent me back some excellent pictures which will be great for her book.'

Sam's biggest design challenge was an oral history book printed in English and three different Aboriginal languages, where she had to lay out the text side by side. Late in 1999 she illustrated a children's book entitled *The Best Little Knitter*, and she plans to do more illustration.

Publishing is still in its infancy as far as Australian Aboriginal communities are concerned, according to Sam. 'We have a long way to go with Aboriginal publishing, especially on an international level, like in Canada, New Zealand and North America. Human resources are really limited, so we need to look at how we can support each other on an international level, and maybe put in place joint distribution and look at cross-cultural development from different indigenous communities. It's not just about Aboriginal activism these days, it's about community supporting community and that whole sense of unification and identity which is taking place.'

Each weekend Sam does a voluntary shift on Broome's community radio station, playing black music. She calls her segment The Black Market.

Sam has two children — daughter Madison, born in 1994, and son Carlos, born in 1997. Their father is an American who Sam met while in Los Angeles. They split up soon after Carlos's birth, and she returned to Australia. She is not unhappy about the outcome of the relationship, nor about being a single parent.

'I think I'm the best person for the job at the end of the day. It's not something I think about too hard, because I haven't lost out. I've never had any trouble being a mother, it's been a natural progression for me. I have two little Sams running around! I live with my sister Kylie, who has a son, and the Aboriginal way of family is that my kids are like hers and vice versa. Cousins are considered brothers and sisters. I have lots of family support in terms of childcare. The kids don't get upset if I have to travel, because they have that network around them.'

With the demands of her children and job, Sam's lifestyle is sometimes too busy for her to appreciate her home town. 'I seem to just work and go home,' she sighs. 'I don't realise how good it is living here until I go away. You have the beauty of the environment here. It's not fast paced. I can see the stars here, but I don't look up often enough.'

PALAEONTOLOGIST
Perth, Western Australia
Born: Brighton, England, 1950

Ken McNamara

Boxes of fossils are piled high on the shelves around Ken McNamara's rather cramped office. Hundreds of pieces of rock are laid out on the benches, waiting for closer examination, when they will reveal some more of the earth's secrets. Through the window, the buildings of the Perth skyline peer in at Ken's strange and ancient world, which is still being unearthed.

Ken is Curator of Invertebrate Fossils at the Western Australian Museum, which began as a geological museum in the 1890s. Now renowned as an international centre for geology, the museum holds 1.5 million fossils, which, Ken says, 'is a lot to look after and get to know'. One week's worth of collected specimens can create years of research for someone like Ken, who is one of eight full-time staff in the museum's geology department.

'For each specimen, you have to research the whole area around it,' Ken explains. 'You have to put it in context, figure out if it's new, then formally describe and notate it. Then you look at what interesting patterns are coming out of it. You look at the changing distribution of fossils through time to help reconstruct the past.

'So for silly little boring fossils, they hold the potential to tell a lot about the global story. Most people think: "Yes fossils, they look nice on the mantelpiece," and that's it. But there is so much information locked up in them. They hold the key to patterns of the past and that's what I find fascinating about them.'

Ken's fascination with fossils began early. As a young

child in England he would wander Brighton Beach, finding specimens among the pebbles. He spent his youth playing football and cricket on the streets and only just scraped through school, but he went to Aberdeen University in Scotland, and majored in geology. 'The north of Scotland was our playground. Geologically speaking it was incredibly diverse and we went out every Wednesday in a Land Rover, collecting specimens as well as sampling malt whiskies up and down Scotland.'

From Aberdeen, he went to Cambridge and spent three years there, doing a PhD on trilobites. 'Cambridge really has some of the worst elements of how you imagine the English to be, and these kinds of people concentrate in places like Cambridge. Towards the end of my time there, I couldn't cope with it and thought I'd better get out and go somewhere completely different.'

Ken chose Australia. In 1976, he found a job as a tutor at the University of Queensland in Brisbane. He spent a year there, then a year as a research assistant at Sydney University, before being appointed curator at the museum in Perth.

'After the frenetic energy of Sydney, Perth was peaceful, quiet and like an overgrown village. It was a nice, open, beautiful city you could sink into and relax. It's changed now to a degree, but I think Perth still has that feeling.'

One of Ken's most recent discoveries — a slab of rock with tracks in it, found in the Kalbarri National Park — is the best of his career. 'We found the oldest evidence of animals walking on land. The set of tracks was made by a giant scorpion, about two metres long, and it's 440 million years old. It's the oldest evidence of animals coming out of the water and walking on land, long before vertebrates did. You can work out how the animal moved from its tracks. You get this tiny little snapshot, which represents about forty seconds of this animal's life, of what happened 440 million years ago.'

Ken's research involves a pre-Darwinian concept called the theory of heterochrony, which examines how animals grow up, and the rate at which they change as

they do so. 'What interests me is not what evolved from what, but what the mechanisms are that enabled it to occur. I look at the relationship between how animals change as they grow up, and relate it to evolution.'

Ken's research doesn't focus on genetics, but on changes in timing and growth. 'I get criticised by geneticists,' he admits. 'They say genetic mutation equals change and evolution. I say it's not as simple as this. If the gene that turns on the growth hormone, say to grow an arm, is slightly delayed, then it can have a big effect on what the structure looks like. If it produces something that's more useful, then natural selection will favour it, so you don't need these genetic mutations to make the change.

'There is a genetic basis to it, but some gene may turn on a day later which will have a significant effect on the whole sequence of events. You can relate this to congenital abnormalities that people have, like cleft palate, because the development closure didn't occur when it should have, so a lot of these abnormalities have the same underlying cause as evolutionary changes. By looking at strange fossils from half a billion years ago, I can apply these same things to congenital abnormalities in children.'

If the same trends in human evolution continue, Ken boldly predicts, in a few billion years, we'll be larger, have bigger brains, smaller jaws, and feed off blood. We just won't be around to see if our theories are proved right,' he laughs.

The lack of teaching of earth sciences in Australian schools concerns Ken, a father of three, and convinces him of the need for good museums. 'I think as time goes on museums will be seen to be more important. We're custodians of our cultural and natural heritage and we must preserve these aspects of our past.'

Ken is chuffed that the best-preserved fossil fish in the world, found in the Kimberleys in 1986, is named after him. It is the *Mcnamaraspis kaprios*, the fossil emblem of Western Australia, and features on a postage stamp released in 1997.

FISHERMAN/ RESTAURATEUR

Kalbarri, Western Australia

Born: Geraldton, Western Australia, 1955

'Number eighteen!' Gary Finlay yells from behind the barbecue plate in his fish restaurant. The customer emerges, takes his plate of freshly cooked tuna and chips, grabs some cutlery, the roll of toilet paper on offer instead of serviettes, and seats himself at one of the wooden tables by the open fire. This is Finlay's Fresh Fish Barbecue, a quirky outdoor restaurant where you eat your ten-dollar plate of barbecued seafood amid a strange collection of nautical paraphernalia. If you can entertain with music or song, you eat for free.

Situated in a quiet back street in Kalbarri, a coastal community on the edge of a national park, the restaurant was originally a fish supply and processing depot, managed by Gary. He set up the depot in 1983 after moving from his home town of Geraldton, where he had spent his life fishing. Gary's father Harry was a fisherman and as a youth Gary remembers being fascinated by the 'comradeship and charm' of the fishing industry.

'Actually I never wanted to be a fisherman,' Gary admits. 'I used to get sick as a dog on the boat. I was about fourteen or fifteen and it was just a run of the mill thing then, when you had to go out and work for your old man. You didn't get paid but you got fed and looked after. From there it grew on me. It was hard work, but it was free and easy.'

Gary was sixteen when his father was badly burned in a backyard accident. He found himself skipper of the fishing boat by the time he was seventeen. 'The Department of Marine and Harbours knew about me. They just kept an eye on me to make sure I was doing the right thing, and they left me alone,' he says.

The early 1970s were the good old days of commercial crayfishing, when most of it was being exported to the USA. Competition between fishermen was lively, but big catches were easy, according to Gary, and there was also a spirit of co-operation. 'Nowadays the crayfish industry is pretty bitchy. In those days, people would help each other — like one bloke, he loaned someone a sail once, which is the equivalent today of lending someone a $50,000 motor. We built pots for people who couldn't afford it. Now, if we were out in the ocean where someone needed quick assistance, people would be unwilling to stop and help. I can remember in Geraldton, you'd see a flare on the horizon and see fifteen boats go straight in to help.'

The ocean was more generous in his early fishing days, too. He remembers a trip north to Shark Bay, where the fish were plentiful. 'There were no boats up there at the time. Everything I did was not influenced by other elements, it was just me and nature. If you

made a mistake, you had time to work out what you did wrong, because there were no other fishermen. It was pioneering stuff.'

The solution to the depletion of fish stocks is to stop fishing in the breeding season, according to Gary. 'The sea is very sustainable. The politicians hand us all these suggestions, which are just paper games. They're not doing the simple thing, which is going back to the beast and discovering that we need to rebreed. Confirmation of this is in aquaculture. When you start an aquaculture project, you never kill off your adult stock, you always breed off the juvenile stock.

'If we go out fishing today and pull up a seven-kilogram snapper and bring him back and open him up, we might find two and a half kilograms of spawn in it — how many million eggs is that? You put a little fish back, and he suffers more stress and trauma in recovering from it, while a lot of the big ones, when they get away, they'll swim away unharmed. You're better to fish inside shallow ground and let the breeding happen in deeper ground. You can't get bureaucracy and the fishermen all to bite the bullet and agree on one simple thing.'

In the Easter of 1978, Gary pulled into the jetty at Kalbarri for the first time to sell fresh fish from his boat. 'We started cooking it in the wheelhouse so customers could sample it. We were doing the full-on sales pitch but in a real primitive way, like half the crew would be hungover from the night before.

'Some of the cuisine talents your deckies developed with seafood over the years was truly amazing. They were bloody useless cooks on land, but put them out to sea for six days and they were great. As fishermen we had the privilege of tasting fish how it should be, but when you passed it on to someone else to sell it, then someone else to cook it, all the links in your chain were thrown out the window. This caused the fish industry to have a bad name.'

After establishing the fish depot in 1983, Gary worked on developing export markets by changing the way the fish was gutted, stored and transported. He believes he was the first fish supplier in the country to sell fish killed in the Japanese 'iki jimie' style — speared in the head, then immediately iced to retain as much freshness as possible. Selling interstate and overseas was the only way he could break away from the Perth domestic market and make some money, because 'fishing was a real pauper's game'.

By 1987, the depot employed forty people and produced 400 tonnes annually, eighty-five per cent of which was being flown overseas or around the country. It had also won an award for small business of the year. But disaster soon struck, with strikes in 1988 by air traffic controllers and transport workers, then again in 1989, with a national pilots strike that lasted eleven months. Within a few weeks of the pilots going on strike, Gary's business had almost been brought to a standstill.

'At any one time, we would have between $20,000 and $30,000 of product somewhere in transit,' Gary explains. 'That product, which had been processed to exact specifications, would be sitting in a chiller somewhere in an airport. Every time there was a delay, it would cost us $30,000 because the fish would be spoiled and destined for the tip.'

With a cool room full of fish that wasn't going anywhere, Gary put up notices around town inviting people to a cheap seafood barbecue and fish filleting demonstration. He figured it was the only way to get rid of the fish. Only three people turned up the first night, but by the third night, with local sympathy for Gary's predicament spreading, he was cooking for a crowd. 'It reminded me of the stories of early Australia, when the country stuck together,' Gary recalls. 'They were good slabs of fish we were cooking up really cheap, and it soon spread like wildfire.

'Our creditors were screaming for our money, and we could have done the easy thing, like most of Australia did, and go bankrupt, but in the fishing industry the people you dealt with were always regarded as friends, so we just decided to knuckle down and trade our way out of it.' And so Finlay's Fresh Fish Barbecue was born.

With finances stretched, Gary used old ice-box lids and fish crates for tables, and transformed the depot into a restaurant with every nautical item he'd collected over the years. 'I was brought up being told not to chuck anything away because you might use it one day. This place carries the Australian hallmark of three-inch nails and barbed wire,' he laughs.

Ten years on, the restaurant is a very successful town institution. Gary finds time to fish in the mornings, but spends most of his day running the restaurant and is happy to buy most of his fish from the local fishermen.

In some respects, he is grateful for the pilot's strike. It gave him a business he never expected to have. 'This place is an extension of fishing really,' says Gary. 'The satisfaction I've got out of it is unbelievable.'

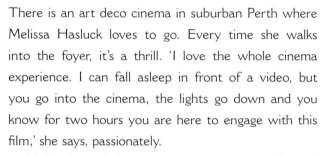

FILM-MAKER
Perth, Western Australia
Born: Perth, Western Australia, 1965

There is an art deco cinema in suburban Perth where Melissa Hasluck loves to go. Every time she walks into the foyer, it's a thrill. 'I love the whole cinema experience. I can fall asleep in front of a video, but you go into the cinema, the lights go down and you know for two hours you are here to engage with this film,' she says, passionately.

Melissa's stepfather was station manager at Channel 7 in Perth, which meant she was exposed to a lot of film and television from an early age. 'We were one of the first houses in the street to get colour TV. When they bought their movie of the week for the TV station, they were on sixteen millimetre, so we brought them home and watched them as a family. I saw all the old films — the Cecil B. De Mille epic classics, like *The Bible*, and *Cleopatra*, and favourites, like *Bonnie and Clyde* and *Bridge over the River Kwai*. I was pretty obsessed with films but I always thought it was something other people did, and within WA there wasn't a visible film industry.'

Melissa was twenty-five and studying journalism part-time while working in an antiques and interiors business when she decided she wanted to be a film-maker. 'There was a visiting tutor from the documentary industry who encouraged me to go out and do it. I never had it in myself to say: "Yeah I can do this." I needed someone to tell me,' she admits.

'Then two girlfriends and I decided to take four weeks off and make a road movie travelling across

166

Australia, using a Video Eight. We got picked up by the police so many times because we all looked a bit crazy. We were body painted as Matisse, Van Gogh and Magritte paintings, hitching along the road after running out of petrol. We vogued in the desert by the light of car headlights wearing coloured skivvies, pre *Priscilla, Queen of the Desert* and pre Wiggles. Some excerpts from that first film ended up in another short film that the same two friends and I made together for a Sydney exhibition of works. This film was inspired by the road trip, surrealism and crotcheted rugs, and the audience loved it. The first road movie is one we look back on and laugh about. One day it'll be a cult classic,' she jokes.

Melissa moved to Melbourne to get a graduate diploma in film and television from Swinbourne Institute (now Victorian College of the Arts) and then began the long haul of nudging her way into a tight and competitive industry. 'I was a runner on a telemovie, then production secretary on a feature film. I got lots of little jobs, but it's hard to get anything because there's a lot of people vying for experience. You have to put yourself forward to work for free. You have to work on a lot of low-budget, student or self-funded projects, so that eventually people recognise that you have some experience.'

With the film business in Melbourne suffering badly from the recession, Melissa reluctantly returned to Perth at the end of 1992. 'Perth didn't seem to be reeling so much. Things seemed easier here and automatically I started getting some jobs and experience, and it fell into place, so I stayed.'

Since 1992, Melissa's work has included a documentary about her grandfather, Paul Hasluck, and his work in archiving the civil history of the war; a six-part series, *Artists Upfront*, about contemporary Aboriginal artists, commissioned by SBS television; and a one-hour documentary with Paul Roberts and Des Kootji Raymond, called *Buffalo Legends*, which was a social history of Darwin using a football team called the Buffalos as a vehicle.

'This footy team was started by an Aboriginal person and from it a whole social movement for equality and justice came about. The program looked at mixed race people being institutionalised and how it dispersed family solidarity and culture. This was one of those experiences when I thought: "How lucky am I, to do the work I do and be exposed to these kinds of people, and to be able to help bring their stories to a wider community?"'

Melissa was third assistant director on a film called *Under the Lighthouse Dancing*, which was her first mainstream commercial film. 'Films are very hierarchical — which is one of the things I don't like about film — so on this one I was the lowest shitkicker,' she laughs. Following this, she was second assistant director on a telemovie called *Heat* and also worked on *Sweat*, a television series about a sports institute.

The fickle nature of the industry means that Melissa's income is always inconsistent. 'With emerging film-makers — which I consider myself — it's a struggle,' she admits. 'Even for some feature-film producers, I'm sure there are periods where times are tight.'

In the past three years, Melissa has been working in partnership with another film-maker, Melanie Rodriga, on developing drama projects. They work from home, and call themselves Cecile B. deux Mels. In 1999, she was granted a new producer's fellowship, which provides her with an allowance to develop industry attachments. She was also producing and casting a three-part drama series commissioned by SBS and Screen West, called *Christina's Birthday*.

'It's a cross-cultural romantic comedy with a twist, and a story that contains a uniquely Western Australian perspective. Western Australia is really isolated, and I think we are informed by this isolation and space around us. There is a sense of space and lightness here which I think is unique,' Melissa says thoughtfully.

She is now moving away from documentaries and towards drama, with the long-term ambition of making feature films. Much of her time is spent in creative

development and planning of various projects. 'When you're running your own business there is so much to do, especially when you are juggling six or seven projects at once. At the end of a week, no-one hands over a cheque and says, "You're worth this much." You have to be really self-motivated and with all the challenges, you never get bored.'

Melissa feels there are more opportunities for her on the west coast than the east. The WA documentary industry is strong and vibrant, with a history of award-winning programs, and the WA film industry is growing, but it's also erratic. 'Over in the East, every second person is a film-maker or a wannabe film-maker. There are a lot more people vying for the pool of money there.'

While she misses the reality of documentary making, Melissa hopes she can convey important stories to the wider community through drama and films.

'I'd like to be at a stage where we're producing a feature film every two years. It's frustrating that in this industry, things take so long to happen. When I look back I think I haven't done much yet, but then I have done lots of interesting things, all of which have brought me to who I am now, and I can put those experiences into my work. You work on things because you need the money or the experience, but you do this because you hope you can eventually work on things that really matter. I'd like to have enough credibility eventually to be able to do this.'

WEATHER OBSERVER
Eucla, Western Australia
Born: Sydney, New South Wales, 1964

Adam Jauczius

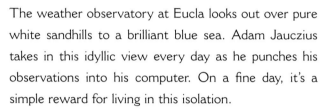

The weather observatory at Eucla looks out over pure white sandhills to a brilliant blue sea. Adam Jauczius takes in this idyllic view every day as he punches his observations into his computer. On a fine day, it's a simple reward for living in this isolation.

Perched on the edge of the Nullarbor, just shy of the South Australian border, Eucla has a population of sixty-five. There's not much to the town, aside from a hotel and caravan park, a police station, an agriculture office and a few houses. Adam has been stationed in Eucla since 1995. He has quite happily spent his career as a weather observer in transit, moving to a new location every three years or so. Some of these places have been small, remote communities.

'There are many good things about living in a small place that you have to sacrifice if you go to a big place,' says Adam. 'Like if I just want to nip home, it only takes me one minute. You get to see a hell of a lot more of your family. There's more community spirit in a town like this. The job is fantastic, because it gives you the opportunity to see a wide range of Australia without having to travel. You go to a place, you settle there and you get to really soak it in.'

Frequent moves and isolated towns are familiar to Adam. When he was five or six, his father worked at the tracking station at Woomera Island Lagoon, a community with 5000 resident Americans. After moving towns several times during his youth,

he finished high school in Adelaide, and in 1983 scored a traineeship with the Bureau of Meteorology in Melbourne. It involved nine months of intensive training, followed by three months probationary duties at a weather station, after which he could be permanently assigned to a station.

'I applied to go to the West. I wanted to work in South Australia, but it was locked out, and Tassie was no go — observers went there to die!' he explains. Adam and his new wife Jenny — his high school sweetheart, who he married during his training — spent some time in Meekatharra, then Perth, before being posted to Forrest, on the old Nullarbor Plain railway line. 'We were there two years and we loved it. The "tea and sugar" train was still running and the fettlers' camp was still there. There were four families working for the Bureau and five families with the railways. Nobody had any kids, and we had parties and barbecues all

the time. You could just jump on a train and go somewhere if you wanted.'

The couple returned to Perth for four years while Jenny did some university study, relocated to Carnarvon for three-and-a-half years, then moved to Eucla. Being in one station for too long, especially an isolated one, 'can send you troppo', Adam says. His method of staying sane is to take a decent holiday away from the place and return refreshed.

Weather observers are divided into two groups — those who roam, like Adam, and those who stay put. Most of the larger coastal towns and cities are considered permanent postings, while those in the interior are transitory. 'Usually these ones are in the towns that aren't considered "nice", so they give you incentives, like they make the rent free and give you an allowance,' Adam explains.

Adam's seven-day-a-week job involves gathering

data, not forecasting. He has witnessed the enormous impact of new technology on meteorology. 'Our job has been halved by automation. When I first joined in 1983, the most advanced piece of equipment was a telex machine. There were no photocopiers, fax machines, computers, printers or answering machines. All the things we did were done manually, like putting weather balloons up and monitoring rainfall. Now they're all programmed to be done electronically. It's just astounding the amount of change that has occurred.'

The general public has become more weather conscious as a result of changing technology, too. 'No-one knew the Bureau existed before,' Adam comments. 'There is a public relations aspect to it now. It wants to make the public aware that it's not just something on at the end of the news, it's actually a very intense program that goes on all over the world. To the public, I guess, it's only how hot or cold it will be, or if their wedding or party will be disturbed by rain, but to industries like mining and aviation, it's absolutely crucial because they need to know certain things.'

Adam and Jenny have two children, and Jenny, a qualified teacher, is home schooling Katherine, aged seven. 'We started by doing School of the Air. Katherine was reading and writing at five, so when she started with School of the Air, it was too basic for her. We thought they'd modify the program, but they didn't, they just kept on giving her the old stuff, so in the end we came up with our own program, and she's really flourishing with it. We'll do the same with our son Jack, too, regardless of where we are.'

Living in Eucla has some disadvantages as far as their children are concerned. 'We will move again, because it's important for kids to interact with other children, and those opportunities are very limited here at the moment.'

Obviously, social interaction for Adam and Jenny is also limited here. 'You've got to make friends. You don't make enemies because you can't afford it!' laughs Adam. 'It's harder for single people out here. They are more or less forced to socialise at the pub every night. Because I'm in a family arrangement, it's not that difficult. You do crave anonymity sometimes and just want to melt back. I would not advocate spending all your time here, or you would go crazy. When people are getting under your skin, it's time to get out. You go and visit your friends or family, then come back again.'

Adam spends much of his spare time painting. After watching his mother and grandmother paint and trying to imitate them, he only took up the brushes seriously again in 1989. He uses pastels and oils and mostly paints landscapes, sometimes portraits. He regularly exhibits his work in a Perth gallery. 'I often think: If only I could paint something as you really see it. The beauty of this land isn't obvious out here — there is just a whole lot of sky and a whole lot of horizon. I try to capture this by being faithful to what I see.'

'Living here and coping is all to do with your own personal outlook. I've always had a very basic outlook on life and any decision I make is based on a simple premise: If you have a solid family life, it doesn't matter where you are. It's the simple things I like — painting, gardening — and you don't have to be anywhere to enjoy them.'

RETIRED BUILDER
Kudardup, Western Australia
Born: Forban, England, 1920

Harry Challis often enjoys the short stroll from his home, down his driveway and through a paddock to reach the Blackwood River that flows alongside his lush land. When his family first arrived here from England in 1923, the bush was so dense that it took his father two weeks to find the river.

Enticed by the 'land of milk and honey' image of Australia portrayed in England, Harry's father, a farm manager, chose to emigrate as part of the group settlement scheme. The idea of the scheme, introduced by WA premier Sir James Mitchell in 1921, was to start a profitable dairy industry in the south-west of Western

Australia by using British migrants to clear and develop the land. Approximately 6000 migrants were selected for this south-west pocket.

The Challis family was alloted 176 acres at Kudardup, just north of Augusta. Five settlers were grouped together; each of them cleared twenty-five acres on each allotment, and was provided with a very basic house, six cows and tools. But once the property was developed, it was valued, and the settlers had to pay back a percentage to the Agricultural Bank. 'They paid us three pound something a month to live on but from there you had to scratch out a living on your own,' Harry explains. 'Everything they supplied you with — tools, cows etc. — were all debited against the property.

'We were very fortunate we had the fish in the river because we went out on a boat and caught them, then sold them to all the other settlers. Any fish you could think of came out of that river. Dad was a great gardener, so we always had plenty of vegies, and Mum was a marvellous cook — she had cooked in big houses in England. Though I might not have had a pair of shoes until I was about ten, I never knew what it was to be hungry.'

Harry vividly remembers the crude four-room humpy he and his eight siblings called home. 'The weatherboards, six-by-ones, as we called them then, were just green off the saw and the floors weren't nailed down. You could look through from one room to the other because the boards shrank up so much.'

Restored original settlement cottage in Kudardup

With the area inundated by British children like himself, Harry relished his early years. There were forty children in the local school, most of them British. 'We made our own lifestyle. We used to trap possums and go fishing. We knocked a canoe out of a sheet of corrugated iron. Every weekend we would help clear the paddocks and pick up sticks. Everybody was the same round here, we only had a horse and cart.'

By the time the Depression hit in 1931, the Challis farm was one of the showplaces of the district. Although it was the smallest of the whole group, its orchard and riverside location made it more valuable. When the farm was valued and Harry's father couldn't pay the forty pounds interest, the bank took the new

heifers instead. 'We couldn't make a living, so they foreclosed on him and we went out in the cold wicked world, right into the Depression,' says Harry, grimly.

Having lost the farm, most of the family moved to Perth. Harry was thirteen when he found his first job milking cows, working seven days for ten shillings a week. He spent the next two years roaming around the south-west, doing a range of farm jobs. 'I had very little schooling in my life but those first two years I spent working, I learned the value of life, and it was better than university,' Harry says. 'I had so many different jobs that I thought: "Bugger this, I have three older brothers, none of them have a trade, so I'm going to get a trade." I was looking to the future.'

Harry found a trade as a plasterer and got a five-year apprenticeship. He earned eighteen shillings and tuppence a week, gave his mum ten shillings of it and used the rest to buy tools and clothes. In 1939 he volunteered to do construction work at the Larrakeyah Barracks in Darwin. 'There was no plastering to do, so I became a rigger, a carpenter, you name it — until we could do the plastering.'

Fortunately, all Harry's efforts to become a soldier failed. 'I tried to join up and was told they had plenty of soldiers, that they needed builders. Then they wanted volunteers to go to Malaysia to build this hospital, and we were all ready to go when the Japanese moved in and cancelled it out. I would have been a POW, for sure.'

By 1942 Harry's mother, a rather astute businesswoman, had made a conditional purchase on a block of land next door to the original group settlement block. She wanted to see Harry and another son, Dave, use it for dairy farming, and they fulfilled her wishes. 'We were classed as primary producers, so when I tried to sign up for the war again, they wouldn't let me because they needed primary producers,' Harry smiles.

The following year, he married Mary, also a British migrant. He also decided to leave the farming to his brother and return to building. He began as a builder's labourer, and business steadily increased. 'After the war they brought in this War Service land settlement, and all these farms in the area were allocated to ex-servicemen. All the homes were the same. They were labour-only contracts, and they'd just give you the plans and supply the materials. I was getting 450 pounds per house. We were building lots of them.'

For many years Harry was the only registered builder south of Busselton. His slogan was: 'If you want a palace, you must see Challis.' As the population increased, so did the workload. At one time, Harry had built about eighty per cent of Augusta — the post office (his address has been PO Box 1 ever since), all the churches bar one, the hotel, and numerous homes. 'I used to work seven days a week because I was doing all my own plans and specifications. I was seeing clients, doing all the ordering — it was full on. It got to the stage where I was laying bricks myself. I laid every brick in the first four motel units in the Augusta Hotel-Motel.'

The 1950s and 1960s were boom times for Harry, and as his business thrived, he took on a number of apprentices and labourers. One of his brothers was a cabinet-maker, and worked for him for thirty-two years. 'I had a terrific team, who were good workers. We were the Challis gang and on Friday nights we'd fill the bar. We had our own dart team — the chippies team.'

By some sort of divine justice, the original group settlement homestead and land came back on the market in 1976, and the Challis family snapped it up at a cost of 30,000 pounds. 'We paid 12,000 pounds up front, then the remainder at six per cent interest. So after all those years, we finally got the house back,' Harry laughs. Four of his brothers returned to live in the same area, and the Challis family now owns a total of 600 acres in Kudardup.

Harry and Mary had four children. Their son Jim, who lives next door with his family, is a registered builder, while their other son Robert is a bricklayer. Harry's home is built in the shape of an H. The original homestead is still on the block, but is unoccupied.

Harry retired from building in the mid 1980s. At the age of eighty, he remains very active, still fishing and tending some beef cattle on his property. 'I haven't really got any regrets because I've had a good life. I don't think I could have gone into anything better. I couldn't have done office work.

'I was supposed to retire at the age of fifty-nine, and that year we went on a *Women's Weekly* world cruise for four-and-a-half months. I came back so satisfied that I was in the best country in the world, in the best state, and the best spot right here on the Blackwood. I came back so contented that I felt like a millionaire in my own right. You can take me out in a box from here. I want to stay here until I have to go.'

Donna Selby

FOREST RESCUER
Kent River, Western Australia
Born: Gosford, New South Wales, 1961

Two young dishevelled heads emerge from the car buried in the mud beneath the protest pyramid at the entrance to the logging coupe in the Swarbrick State Forest. They have slept inside the car overnight, chained to the car body, prepared for any loggers who might try and gain access to the forest they are trying to protect.

The other members of the protest camp emerge from their tent and light a fire to boil a billy. It's been a cold and very wet night, and the mud is inescapable, but they have no plans to abandon their post. Donna Selby, an environmental activist from the South Coast Environment Group, arrives with a few supplies, having driven from her home in Kent River, about thirty kilometres away. She is here to talk tactics with the logging protesters — or forest rescuers, as they prefer to be known.

This particular section of old-growth forest, containing Yellow Tingle and Karri trees, had been partially clear-felled before the rescuers arrived. 'There is less than 7000 hectares of old-growth Yellow Tingle and Karri forest left on the planet,' Donna explains, with a sense of urgency. 'Under the State Government's Regional Forest Agreement, forty per cent of our remaining Tingle and Karri will be clear-felled and most of the Tingle from this coupe will end up as woodchip. It's just criminal. They say this timber doesn't have a marketability, but Yellow Tingle is a beautiful timber.

We've used it in the stairs in our house. It's one of the hardest woods you can find.'

Donna's passion for her cause pours out of her in fast, confident, articulate speech. She has been devoted to it for several years now, and is often called upon to speak with the media. The necessary facts and figures are always at her fingertips. 'Japan uses plantation trees for first-grade pulp. They don't cut down their old-growth forests. Japan has more forest than we have left in Western Australia. Our old-growth Karri and Marri forest timber goes to Japan as seventh-grade woodchip and there are only eight grades! It gets used for low-grade paper and cardboard products,' she explains, hardly pausing to take a breath. 'Even Conservation and Land Management (CALM) and Wesfarmers Bunnings (timber company) admit that sixty per cent of old-growth forest ends up as woodchip. They take that figure from the log landings, not the trees standing, so we figure eighty per cent goes to the chipper.'

Donna first came to the south-west of Western Australia in 1983. She moved from Perth to Kent River in 1992, with her husband, Steve, a carpenter. 'When I first came down here, I fell in love with the place. I don't think I'd ever experienced tall forests before and it just grabbed hold of my heart.'

The conservation movement in the area was very active and Donna soon became aware of it. 'You hit a certain stage of your life and think: "Well all this stuff is happening around me, I want to do something about it." I started fundraising for forests, then I thought I'd better get out and have a look at what I was fundraising for, then before I knew it, I was sitting out in the middle of a road blockade with (my daughter) Tammy, who was eight months old. We used to pack up our breakfast and head out at four or five in the morning and sit out on the roads, and it all evolved from there. The first time I saw a clear-fell and the burnt logs that could have been

used, I thought I had to do something, even if it was only a little.'

Donna came to the forefront of her environment group in 1995, when it was involved in a major campaign to stop logging in Sharpe Forest, also in the south-west. Prior to this, logging protesters had been generalised as 'feral', but Donna believes this image has since changed.

'I became spokesperson in this campaign, because I was the only one who didn't mind putting on a suit and going on camera. At the time, we tried to consciously change the feral tag. We knew mainstream society wouldn't get involved if we didn't change the image. You used to think ferals, but it's not the case anymore, it's the city suburbia set. Now we have shire presidents getting arrested for the forests, and people like Liz Davenport (fashion designer), and retired surgeons. The voice of protest is more mainstream, which is why I think we're winning.'

In 1998, Donna's South Coast Environment Group put their Walpole Wilderness Proposal to the WA government. It offered local solutions to the logging dispute, and represented two years of work for Donna, but it was basically ignored when the government drew up its Regional Forest Agreement. However, Donna had her most public moment of glory when she gatecrashed the event at which WA Premier Richard Court officially signed the agreement. Angry about certain aspects of it, and believing she had been betrayed by the environment minister, Donna decided to make her views known.

'I came from the back of the room yelling: "It's a sham." The triumph of my life was that I got to stand in front of this politician and say: "You lied to me." Richard Court ran from the podium, so I thought, "There's my spot", and I gave a spiel about the government ripping off the public before security dragged me out of the room. It made the national news that night,' she says proudly.

Donna says while she never acts out of anger, it is her anger about the destruction of the forests that sustains her. 'There's so much beauty wrapped up in old-growth forest and to go back and see it as a graveyard, it makes your blood boil.'

Saving the trees is not just about preserving beauty, however. Donna believes the only way to save the forests is to convince the government of the economic good in it and to promote their ecological necessity. 'Australia is this big arid country, but down here in the south-west we have this moist pocket. We all know trees attract rain, so what will happen if we change the ecology of this area is that it will impact on our weather system. The forests are the lungs of our earth, they are of huge scientific research value. They have secrets in them that we haven't even discovered yet.

'Here in Walpole we have 230,000 tourists coming down to see the Valley of Giants (a bushwalk through tall forest) each year. If we can offer them an environment-based experience, we can encourage those people to linger longer. Eco-tourism is the fastest-growing industry we've got and it's semi-sustainable. If we do have a timber industry, let's have one that's sustainable, based on plantations, that values forest products, so we fell on a smaller aerial basis and everything felled in a forest gets used.'

Donna spends up to fifty hours a week working in a voluntary capacity for the environment group. She is planning on setting up a home business — a wildflower garden and cafe — within the next few years, but for the moment, her priority is saving the forests.

Her vision for the future of the planet remains positive, but she would like to see more people become involved in protecting the environment at a local level. 'There's so much happening that people often feel daunted by the hugeness of it. I think there is hope. If there wasn't hope, I wouldn't have had kids. I think we need to work on individuals empowering themselves to act. If we can collaboratively do something, then we will have an effect. We need governments with an environmental conscience.'

PILOT
Kununurra, Western Australia
Born: Wangaratta, Victoria, 1972

Michael Fleming

It's just on sunrise, and Michael Fleming is doing the first flight of the day over the East Kimberleys, Bungle Bungles and Lake Argyle in his single-engine Cessna 207. Beneath the hum of the plane is the buzz of his passengers, excited by the view. Below are the awesome red beehive-like mounds of the Bungle Bungles, which until the early 1980s, remained largely unknown to the general public. Now, several tourist flights pass over these spectacular ranges and Lake Argyle, a 1000 square kilometre inland sea, every day.

'You've got to be mad to sit in one of these things for two hours, but people really enjoy it,' he admits. Today, Michael will spend just two hours flying and the rest of the day in his overalls, doing plane maintenance for Alligator Airways.

With a high demand for tourist flights over the Bungle Bungles and Lake Argyle, the remote town of Kununurra is a training ground for would-be commercial pilots, who need to accumulate flying time. Michael is in this category. During a four-year aircraft engineering apprenticeship with Qantas in Sydney, he used his wages to take flying lessons, always aiming to become a pilot. He completed the apprenticeship at age twenty-two, but continued working for Qantas until he was twenty-six, then moving to Kununurra.

Michael's father is a pilot, and a very strong influence in his life. 'I always wanted to be like him,' he says. 'I was a crazy little aeroplane child — I had a plane mobile

over my cot at three months old and as a boy, I would walk around making aeroplane noises. I've lived under a flight path all my life.' Up until the age of eight, Michael would accompany his dad in his twin-engine plane on charter flights between Wangaratta and Melbourne.

Michael's future career was decided well before he finished high school. 'I knew what I wanted to do, but didn't know how I was going to get there. I had done work experience in a plane hangar in school, then one day Mum put the ad in front of me for Qantas. I did an aptitude test and a medical, then I was in. There were thousands of applicants. It was just after Qantas had been through a rough patch of losing a lot of engineers, so they took on 300 in my year. The first year was all in-house schooling at Qantas. Then I went out to the jet base, with eight weeks of technical college each year.'

Flying felt completely natural to Michael. 'It wasn't a scary thing. When I did my first solo, that was pretty special. I did a circuit over Sydney. Suddenly it was just me out there,' he sighs.

Michael could have gone directly into commercial flying by paying $100,000 to do pilot training with Qantas. Besides not being able to afford it, he doesn't consider this an honourable way of learning to fly. Although he knew he needed to spend more time flying to qualify for the major airlines, he spent another four years as an engineer to secure his finances. 'I didn't want to come up here with debts hanging over my head,' he says.

When Michael and his fiance, Elizabeth Armstrong, first arrived in Kununurra in February 1999, they went into culture shock. Elizabeth, who is a nurse, had been somewhat reluctant to relocate, but she agreed to it for the sake of Michael's career. Michael had not been able to secure a job in Kununurra, but they left the comfortable familiarity of their lives in Sydney anyhow, hopeful that a position would come up.

'Originally we thought we'd go to Darwin, but then we heard about this town, the Bungle Bungles and the tourists. We heard twenty to thirty pilots were employed here for five months of the year, so the feedback was more positive. Neither of us knew what Kununurra was. We just knew it was hot and pretty small and in the north of WA, that's all,' Elizabeth explains.

They spent the first two weeks picking bananas, and living in a tent in a caravan park. Being the wet season, it rained constantly, which tested their patience.

'We thought Michael might have to spend twelve months working odd jobs before he even got a job,' says Elizabeth. 'But he got offered the job with Alligator Air almost straightaway.'

Michael is earning three-quarters of what he earned as an engineer in Sydney and is finding the cost of living in Kununurra more expensive. 'The rent prices are horrendous — we pay only $5 a week less than what we paid in Sydney. Plus petrol and groceries cost more here.'

I said to him: "You couldn't even say that where I come from." He said: "Well this is Kununurra, I can say what I want!" But every day Michael is a tangible step closer to the big dream, to the big picture.'

While Michael has adjusted more easily than Elizabeth, he says it's a difficult industry to work in, especially in a location such as Kununurra. 'You get treated like crap because there are so many of you — pilots are a dime a dozen here. It's not that I get treated badly by the employers, but considering the job that you do — flying people around — it's not great. There's no glamour in it whatsoever.'

Michael needs to accumulate a minimum of 1,500 hours flying time before he can apply to a major airline. 'I came from an airline and I want to go back to one, because it's damn good working for an airline,' he says with a smile. 'I don't know how to explain flying, I just love it. Being up there and looking at things from a different angle — it's great.'

Elizabeth chose not to nurse and instead found casual work in a bakery, and as a house cleaner. She admits she is having enormous trouble adjusting to life in the town, and feels extremely homesick for Sydney. Her priority for their time here is self-preservation. 'I feel like a lost city girl,' she sighs. 'I feel like living here, especially as a woman, is a step back into the 1960s. The mindset of the businesses is behind the times. I worked for a hotel here, and the guy told me he would never employ a male at the front desk. I almost fell of my chair.

DIDGERIDOO MAKER

Katherine, Northern Territory

Born: Willaroo Station, Northern Territory, 1931

Wearing his weathered hat, Bill Harney is sitting at a rickety old kitchen table, painting a jabiru on a new didgeridoo with his grand-daughter looking on. His hands, more weathered than his hat, tell the story of a life in the bush, of a life spent working. One of thousands of Aboriginal people to work on the outback stations, he has spent most of his life working for others.

Bill's father was a white man, also called Bill. He was the first ranger at Ayers Rock, from 1957 to 1962. As a child, Bill spent little time with his father, because his mother was Aboriginal. 'My mother raised me in the bush,' he explains. 'For a white man to be associated with an Aboriginal woman was considered bad. They (the government) brought all this British law with them, so they took the part-Aboriginal kids away to schools and never sent them back. My mother, she hid me. My father believed that if he took me with him, I would lose my culture, but if I stayed, I would hang on to my culture.'

Bill never went to school, and spent the first forty-eight years of his life at Willaroo, a large cattle station owned by the Besties Company which had about 500 workers and 40,000 head of cattle. 'I worked on the station doing all kinds of jobs — it was our education — like fencing, branding, sinking wells, yard building, breaking in animals and blacksmithing. I was getting 50 cents a week at first. Half of Australia was owned by Besties then — they had big shipping depots and meat works everywhere.'

The last time Bill saw his father was in 1960, when they had dinner together in Mataranka. 'He gave me 100 pounds to help me buy a block of land, which was a lot of money in those days. He wouldn't let me pay him back. "I didn't give you anything," he told me, "because you grew up without me." I didn't learn anything from him. I just learned things myself and from other people.'

One of Bill's earliest memories is watching the elders make and play didgeridoos in the traditional manner. Usually, the branches used to make them are hollowed out by termites. 'They would use stone axes, and spinifex wax to seal the hole, which sets like cement, then a soft wax on the mouth hole. We used to cut

up little sticks and muck around with them. We just picked up on how to play it.'

The didgeridoo is the world's oldest instrument and comes traditionally from the north of Australia. According to Aboriginal tradition, women are not allowed to play it. 'Someone says if a woman starts playing it, she'll have too many kids.'

Katherine was an important crossroad for trading, and Bill says the didgeridoos made at his station were often traded for such things as spears, cooking utensils, and ochres for painting. 'White ochre, like chalk, was from our country and we traded it to the north, south and east. We had the best yellow ochre, and we traded

it, too. The best red ochre came from the desert, so we didn't have this one. Black ochre comes from corkwood bark. You burn the tree, get its fine powder, then mix it to make paint.'

Bill moved to Katherine in 1980, when the town was just 'a dirt street with a couple of stalls, a hotel and that's about all'. He spent six years as a fencing contractor before starting up a business in Aboriginal tours, taking people out to the bush for a taste of indigenous Australian history. 'I show them rock paintings, tell them stories, show them ochre and bush tucker. It's fascinating to people who haven't seen it before,' he says.

Bill spends most of his time living at Innisfail Station,

125 kilometres west of Katherine, but frequently comes in to Katherine to do business and to see his family. He says he doesn't enjoy coming in to Katherine much, and as an elder, is deeply concerned about the effects of alcohol on Aboriginals living in the town.

'People are coming in from the desert, they're being given a house and land to live in but they're not being helped. It doesn't help them go back to the desert. It's forcing Aboriginals into white man's way, and causing anti-social behaviour. When they're sober, they have respect for people like myself, but when they're on the booze, everything is out of hand. We were running a committee to try and stop this behaviour, but no-one would listen to us. Just in town is where the problems are. The proper communities outside the towns work. Tourists don't see the good part, they just see the bad part in the towns,' he laments.

Bill's tours, which came from a desire to show tourists true Aboriginal culture, also led, quite spontaneously, to the didgeridoo making. 'Once when we were out on a tour, camping in the bush, someone suggested playing some music, so I went and got my didgeridoo. Then I cut a fresh stick to make a new one and I was blowing it in the camp and everyone started taking photos of me. I gave that one away. Then, on the next tour, I cut two or three sticks and I got some ochre and started painting them, and they were taking photos again. Then I realised there was money in it and I couldn't keep up with it. I had ten to twenty people at a time coming in and they all wanted a didgeridoo.'

In a didgeridoo market that is now huge, Bill sells about 1000 instruments a year, many of them going to Europe and America. He has scaled down his tourism operation, but still takes small groups out to the bush for two or three day camp-outs as the demand arises. 'The market is getting bigger and bigger. There's a lot of white people starting up factories to make them, but we don't take any notice. There's still quite a few Aborigines making them and they make the best ones,' he smiles.

It takes Bill about two hours to make a didgeridoo and an hour to paint one. Generally, he paints them with his own animal totems — the grasshopper, the wedge-tailed eagle, the jabiru, black and white catfish and the blue crested pigeon.

For Bill, the passing down and the passing on of knowledge is crucial to his people's survival. 'When people come from overseas, they want to learn about Aboriginal culture and history, so we're here to explain it for them. We tell our young ones they have to learn to pass it on to their kids. We got our land, which is the main thing. If we didn't have it, we would be gone. It's important to take the children to our land, to tell them about the place, the songs, the stories of each place.'

LUTHERAN PASTOR
Alice Springs, Northern Territory
Born: Box Hill, Victoria, 1968

Basil Schild

The almost full church empties out with a steady trickle as each member of the congregation stops to greet the two pastors standing either side of the doors. There is an assortment of people filing past the two robed men: quaint elderly ladies in their Sunday frocks; young couples with new babies; laughing, energetic teenagers; serious middle-aged men.

Basil Schild, the younger pastor, speaks kindly with each person as he shakes their hand. His face is youthful, yet his eyes seem to carry all the depth of worldly experience, of a man who has not been sheltered by religious rules. Without his white robes, or the large bronze cross he wears, it would be difficult to pick him as a priest.

Basil was posted to the Alice Springs Lutheran Church in January 1997, his first appointment after completing a theology degree in Adelaide. It was his study of third-world politics for a previous arts degree that led him to theology. 'I was looking at a lot of the revolutions in Latin America, like in Nicaragua, and also in the Philippines. One thing they had in common was a lot of them were led and supported by very passionate people who were extremely religious. I found it interesting because here were people whose religion led them to believe not only in life after death, but in life *before* death. 'So I thought if your religion can bring a passionate ethic for living in the absolute present, then maybe that's not a negative thing.'

Basil first spent time in Central Australia while hitch-hiking around at age eighteen and says returning to Alice Springs was like going home.

'I don't feel like the town is home, but rather the landscape is home. I feel lucky to be here. Everything is close to the edge here. It's a challenge.'

Raised as a Lutheran, with a minister father and a social worker mother, Basil's upbringing was 'religious in a way that led my father and mother to be very passionate about issues of justice'.

The Lutheran Church is the largest Protestant church in the world, but is far more active in the USA and Europe than in Australia.

'We have a strong teaching of the concept of grace,' he begins, in an effort to explain his religion. 'You'll hear this word a lot, grace ... it's the mercy, compassion and forgiveness that is free. It's the sort of message the Lutheran church should be living and dying on, and given with no strings attached. It's a message that God's love is enormous, and overwhelming, and it's free, that you don't have to get your life together first. The first message is that you are loved.'

Basil chooses his words carefully but, as a preacher tends to do, often elaborates at length or draws on Biblical anecdotes to make a point. 'I enjoy the time to think about and reflect on deep issues but not necessarily come up with an answer. I think good questions may be more important than good answers.'

His faith is something he has always questioned, but he considers that a healthy thing. 'Faith is a pretty big word ...' he pauses. 'There's the story of Sarah and Abraham. They're very old and they're promised

a child but that child doesn't come. Finally, God comes and says by the time he comes back next year, there'll be a child. They laugh and they don't believe it's going to happen. Their faith is not strong, but God brings a child anyhow.

'I particularly like the message in 2 Timothy, Chapter 2, verse 13, which you don't hear much, which says: "Even if we are faithless, God remains faithful". You don't hear that much in church. I think if the faith stands up then there's absolutely no fear in questioning it, and if aspects of the traditions of the church don't stand up, then they should be questioned too. I think in our society generally people don't learn to question enough. I'm always amazed at how uncritical people in Australia are. I always thought they were more suspicious of authority, even from the convict thing, but it seems like in the last thirty years it's slipped away and we're just following anything.'

He is critical of new-age spirituality. 'It pushes an inward focus that can be so strong that community becomes secondary. We should be promoting community. Certainly the church of Jesus is founded on the idea of community.'

The church in the Western world is in crisis in terms of its relevance to society, according to Basil, and needs to figure out new ways to communicate its messages to an audience that is no longer listening. 'The church is a bit like a rusty ship with some very good treasures on board. That's one of the reasons I came to work for it. Some of these treasures are extremely valuable to the world for living and it would be a pity if these treasures went down with the ship.'

One-third of Basil's congregation is Aboriginal, an indication of the Lutheran's long-standing presence in Alice Springs and the outlying areas. The Hermannsburg Mission began before the town existed, in 1872. Basil believes that many elements of traditional Aboriginal spirituality can and do exist alongside a Lutheran faith, and is very respectful of ancient beliefs.

'I think the undermining of the original cultures would unfortunately still have happened even if there were no religion, simply through other white culture being brought in. But when the missions ceased to be missions, in the late 1970s and early 1980s, it was discovered that a huge part of traditional culture had continued to be practised over the last century, right through the whole history of the missions.

'People had taken on board spiritual elements that were presented by missionaries but, by the same token, they didn't throw away their own views of spirituality.

As far as I can understand it,' he pauses, 'from the point of view of a dumb whitefella who's only lived here for two years, much of the Dreaming spirituality is still there. The ancestral beings are still a reality for the traditional Aboriginal people who also say they are Christian. The Aboriginals who worship here are here because they identify as part of the Lutheran community and have done so for a long, long time. They would be offended if anyone thought that they were coming not of their own freeness. I think the church — if it thinks its message is important — needs to respect all culture, whether it's indigenous or not. If it wants to be heard, it needs also to listen, rather than ramming its view down peoples' throats.'

Like any pastor, Basil's weekly duties include visiting people, trauma or grief counselling, running Bible discussion groups, attending community meetings, and general church administration. It is the contact with people and the rawness of being involved in their lives that he enjoys most, he says. 'It can be really hard work and I don't think people who are priests choose to do the work because they enjoy it, but this doesn't mean I'd change it.

'It's a beautiful thing to be in church sometimes when you're given the privilege of being so close to people at times of deep emotion. You're let into peoples' lives at times when other people may not be let in. You're around when people are dying and when people are angry at the world. It makes you appreciate the rawness and pain of people and that's what touches me in my work.'

CAMEL FARMER

Kings Creek, Northern Territory

Born: Alice Springs, Northern Territory, 1949

It is 7.15 am and Ian Conway, spatula in hand, is cooking bacon and eggs for the tour group who have stopped at his station for breakfast before visiting nearby King's Canyon. Later today, he'll be rounding up camels and loading them onto a truck to send to market. Like hundreds of outback station owners around Australia, Ian chose to diversify his business to attract the rapidly growing tourist market. For people like Ian, these tourists are generating the income necessary to survive in such remote locations, and he is grateful for their presence. 'We're very fortunate we're on the main tourist route here. Only people on the tourist trail will make ends meet in this country,' he says.

Ian's camel station is 1800 square kilometres — made up of 108 square kilometres of freehold land and 1700 square kilometres of leasehold from the local Aboriginal people. 'I don't like the term "land owner", because I don't think anyone owns land. I'm only here for a short time to look after it, so I'll try and look after it, and when I'm dead and gone, someone else will come and look after it,' he says, matter-of-factly.

The son of a drover, Ian grew up in the bush around Alice Springs. While working as a tour guide and bus driver from Alice, he began catching camels for 'a bit of fun' and giving them away to people. In 1981, he and his wife Lyn took over the government lease on the land to establish Kings Creek station. 'We had no vision of what we were going to do, we knew we just had to make a living out of something, because there were no tourists coming here then. You would have been flat out getting 20,000 or 30,000 people coming through here in a year. This year, we're expecting 250,000. When we first started, Lyn and I did everything ourselves — we did all the building maintenance and we only employed one person for six hours a day.'

A few years after taking over the lease, Ian realised there was a demand for camels overseas and within Australia for tourism, and began catching and selling them. It is estimated there are 200,000 feral camels in Australia. Ian believes he now has anywhere between 200 and 2000 camels on his property, and says camel numbers have only increased since the late 1970s.

'There are about fifty camel farms in Australia now but fifty years ago there were only one or two,' he says. 'Camels are real traffic stoppers. People love them. They've supplied so much to this country without people realising it.'

Ian has developed a healthy respect for the creatures. 'They're a very intelligent animal. In most instances if they're wild they'll protect themselves, like any animal would. If you're gentle to an animal and care for it, you can do anything with them. We try and treat them with tender loving care whenever we can. If you lose your temper with a camel, walk away,' he says, smiling.

With the tourist market saturated, most of Ian's camels are now sold for meat. 'Camel meat only became popular in Australia five years ago, but it's still only a niche market. We can't get them slaughtered, which is the problem. There is only one slaughterhouse in Australia doing camels. Most abattoirs are set up for butchering smaller animals. You get a bull camel weighing a tonne and he's three times as high as a big bullock, which means you have to change the structure of your

abattoirs for health reasons to be able to slaughter them.'

Ian sells between forty and sixty camels a year, most ending up on the supermarket shelves in Adelaide. At current prices, camel meat fetches between 80 cents and $1.10 per kilogram. 'If you have to go out and catch them, it's not great money. The market isn't being promoted simply because we can't provide enough meat. If there were more abattoirs, I'd definitely try and sell more.'

It is the tourist side of the business that keeps Ian and Lyn working so hard seven days a week. Their station sells petrol and take-away food, accommodation for campers and caravanners, as well as serving as a meal stop for tour groups. Ian employs about ten or twelve staff and says one of the things he enjoys most is the comradeship between the workers and himself.

'There's nothing better than the bush to bring everybody to the same level. I like the contact you have with other people, the closeness of everybody who lives in the bush. My family is very close and all our staff become part of the family too.'

Without the support of family, according to Ian, outback life would be even harder. Although he holds no resentment about the lifestyle he has chosen, he describes where he lives as 'the most stressful environment in the country'. 'You take everything for granted in urban situations. If you want water connected, for example, you go and get a plumber to do it. It might cost you $20 for the call-out plus whatever the labour is. If we want a plumber, our call-out fee is $800, just for starters,' he explains.

'Life is tough out here, especially for women. Womenfolk in the bush have played a major role in the development of this country. I say this without any fear whatsoever. Without women in the bush, this country wouldn't have got halfway, where it is now. Apart from being your wife, they're your best friend, a mother to your children, a nurse if you're sick. My daughter is twenty-two years old and there's not a man on this station who can work harder than she can and there's not a man who can show her more than she knows. She can drive anything, ride a motorbike, work in a yard and she knows how to handle cattle and camels.'

Ian is seriously concerned about the number of people giving up life in the bush and moving to the city, and the long-term future of the outback. 'Life is pretty hard out here. Because of financial hardships, falling prices in sheep and cattle, it's up and down all the time. A lot of people out here have worked hard their whole lives, worked their guts out 365 days a year, seven days a week, getting a place up and running, only to get ripped off by agents or bank fees. No-one seems to care what happens in the outback.

'Australians are very backward when it comes to promoting their own country, especially outback Australia, where the guts of this country is. People look at outback Australians as hillbillies, they think because you live out in the bush you know nothing. It is because you live out here that you see and do twenty times more things in a day as what they do in a year.'

SURF LIFESAVER
Darwin, Northern Territory
Born: Melbourne, Victoria, 1966

It is a mid-winter afternoon on Darwin's Casuarina Beach. The temperature is a pleasant 25 degrees Celsius and, although the water looks murky brown and quite uninviting, there are a few brave souls enjoying a dip. From the front of the Casuarina Beach Surf Lifesaving Club, Jo Gardiner is watching some of her fellow clubmates doing some routine training.

Jo holds a unique position in the Australian surf lifesaving movement: she is the only paid surf lifesaving representative in the Northern Territory. There are three patrolled beaches in the Darwin region — Casuarina, Arafura and Gove — and although none of them have surf in the true sense of the word, lifesavers are still a necessity. Between the three beaches, there are approximately 150 lifesavers who give their time voluntarily, most of it in the dry season.

'We do get waves in the cyclone season,' Jo points out in defence of Darwin's waveless beaches, 'so we get to have a bit of a splash around then. I miss the surf, but with this job I get an opportunity to go interstate for the competitions.'

Jo was appointed Development Officer for Northern Territory Surf Lifesaving in 1997. She had previously worked for the Royal Lifesaving Society in Melbourne on an unemployment youth program called LEAP (Landcare and Environment Action Program), which involved six-monthly projects targeted at long-term unemployed youth with low self-esteem.

'Through lifesaving and teaching them to swim, we worked on their self-esteem, leadership skills and how to apply for jobs,' Jo explains. 'There was a lot of recreation and fun involved in it. It was quite successful because somewhere between thirty and forty per cent of kids who went through went on to get jobs, or back to TAFE to study.'

Jo was lifeguarding professionally at Lorne, on Victoria's southern coast, when she made the move to Darwin. She spent her early childhood in Darwin, but her family was forced to return to Melbourne after Cyclone Tracy hit on Christmas Day in 1974. 'I was eight years old when it happened, so it was pretty scary to a kid. Half our house lost the roof. We'd gone to bed and woken in the middle of the night. I remember the Christmas presents not being under the tree anymore.'

Returning to Darwin after twenty-three years away was a refreshing change for Jo. 'Darwin is a really easy lifestyle to fit in to, because there's no hassle. It's so friendly, you walk down the street and everyone says hello, whereas coming from Melbourne, you'd think you were going to be robbed if someone spoke to you. I always thought I was pretty easy-going anyhow, and I guess it's changed me moving here, but I can't say how.'

As a child in Darwin, Jo spent little time at the beach. 'I was in a swimming club at Nightcliff, but I can't recall ever swimming at the beach. We were probably worried about stingers. We did go to the beach, but we never swam there.'

Darwin lifesavers have two deadly beasts to contend with: stingers, or box jellyfish, and crocodiles. The beaches are only patrolled in the non-stinger season, between June and October. For the remainder of the year, the public is advised not to swim. One of Jo's duties is to provide an ongoing public education campaign about stingers.

'Some people will ask about the stingers and some people won't. So it's a constant education process because of the number of tourists coming here. You'll see people go in the water despite a big sign saying there are stingers in the water. If you come from down south, you don't realise the danger. People just think: "How dangerous can a jellyfish be?" They can kill a

child in three minutes, so they're extremely deadly if you get stung badly enough.' The immediate treatment for a sting is vinegar, which kills the tentacles, but an antivenene is required for the injected poison.

'Personally I'd be more scared of stingers here than crocs, but at Gove it's a different story,' Jo explains. 'At Gove it's a routine procedure to take the IRB (inflatable rescue boat) out and look for slides — that is, spots where crocs have slid into the water. They're like a snake line and quite identifiable. I've never heard of a croc taking someone off the beach, but in Gove recently there was a croc chasing some surfers up the beach. During the nipper program, they'll always have a boat in the water or board paddlers looking out. They spotted one once, during a carnival. They still went ahead with it, but made sure they had IRBs in the water. I guess there are sharks out there too, but you don't worry about sharks as much.'

Jo feels privileged because her job encompasses every aspect of lifesaving. In other states, where there are numerous clubs, she would only work in one specific area. 'Because there's only one of you, you have to do everything, from writing up proposals for grants, going to the schools and teaching them about water safety, to running surf carnivals. It's a big learning curve.'

Surf lifesaving everywhere is heavily reliant on volunteers, and in the Northern Territory even more so. Jo believes 'clubbies' are a special class. 'Here, the clubbies pay a fee to join, and they do their bronze medallion, which they also have to pay for. Then they're told they have to do so many hours volunteer work on the beach. It's a certain type of person who's going to give that value back to the community.

'There's a lot of people who do it for recreation and fitness as well as for the social aspect. Once you're a clubbie, always a clubbie,' she smiles. 'You can go to any surf lifesaving club in Australia and tell them you're a clubbie and be accepted. It's like an unwritten rule. There's a camaraderie.'

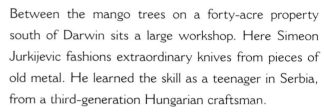

KNIFEMAKER
Acacia Hills, Northern Territory
Born: Subotica, Yugoslavia (Serbia), 1940

Simeon Jurkijevic

Between the mango trees on a forty-acre property south of Darwin sits a large workshop. Here Simeon Jurkijevic fashions extraordinary knives from pieces of old metal. He learned the skill as a teenager in Serbia, from a third-generation Hungarian craftsman.

Simeon remembers a childhood in which, because of the war, he always felt hungry. He grew up in the town of Subotica and got a job in a slaughterhouse at the age of thirteen. His monthly wage was enough to buy one kilogram of pork. After learning knifemaking, he did restoration work in castles, repairing knives, swords, battleaxes and restoring intricate wrought-iron work.

By the time he was twenty-five, Simeon had saved the money he needed for a ticket to Australia. 'I wanted to go anywhere as long as it wasn't Yugoslavia,' Simeon explains. 'I worked in Austria for a year, then I wanted to go away as far as I could. I had an aunty in Mildura, so I went there.'

Simeon speaks Serbian, Hungarian, Polish, Ukranian, Russian and German. When he arrived in Australia in 1966, he spoke these languages to fellow migrants, and says he just 'picked up English from the street'. He found work easily, mainly as a welder, and moved between states for the next four years. At first, he found the freedom to travel surprising. 'Once when I was travelling and approaching the border between Victoria and South Australia, I got my papers ready. I had letters from friends proving who I was and so on.

I got out of the car and there was nobody there!'

In 1969 Simeon met his wife Paulina in Alice Springs when she was working as a nursing sister there. He proposed to her eighteen hours after they first met at a cafe. 'The next day he got all his friends to come and see me at the hospital, and tell me he was a really nice guy,' she laughs.

The couple married in Adelaide in 1970. In 1973 — the same year Simeon became an Australian citizen — they went to live in Nhulunbuy, in Arnhem Land, where Simeon worked as a maintainence fitter at the bauxite mine and Paulina studied to become a teacher. They spent ten years there and loved everything about the place, which Paulina describes as a 'real men's town'. 'You couldn't get bored there,' Simeon says. 'There were plenty of things to do. I had a sailing boat, I went hunting with the Aboriginals, shooting on the shotgun range and bushwalking. It's the best place in the world.'

Simeon's desire to turn his knifemaking hobby into a full-time occupation brought them back to Darwin. They bought two twenty-acre blocks of land for $21,000, and began building the tin-roofed, besser-brick workshop, which, until now, has also sufficed as a house. 'Please do not call this a house. It's a workshop and it looks like one,' Paulina states emphatically. 'We are building a house 360 metres from here. It will be finished one day. We've been building it for three years now. As we get the money, we'll keep building it.'

Paulina teaches primary school in nearby Palmerston and Simeon spends all his time making knives, most of them specially ordered for kitchen or restaurant use, or as collector's items.

Every knife Simeon makes consists completely of recycled materials. Like a blacksmith, he forges and beats the metal to shape the blade. He uses car springs, exhaust valve stems, ball bearings and, for the scabbards, washing machine shells. For the grips, he uses dead timber collected from his property, or the bones

of kangaroos, sheep, camels, dingoes or buffalo horns. He always uses native woods like myrtle, wattle and ironwood, and Australian gems for decorative grips.

'I leave the bones out for the ants to clean up, then polish them up,' he says. 'I recycle everything — I don't buy anything. It's not to save money, because you spend a lot more time working out of something old to make something new than if you bought something new to begin with.' In 1988, he was commissioned to make a set of letter openers for Prince Charles and Princess Diana for their Australian trip. They were made from the recycled exhaust valve stems of a Toyota.

Simeon never advertises, selling all his knives through word of mouth. He has supplied all over the world. In a week, he may make one knife, he may make six, depending on the detail required. His prices range from $50 to $3000, and no two knives are ever the same.

Paulina does all of the intricate etching on the blades.

Knifemaking is not recognised as a profession, which Simeon says has prevented him from getting a bank loan, despite the fact that he has two trade tickets, one as a welder and one as fitter and turner. 'There's no such thing as a knifemaker in Australia, so you can't get a bank loan. I have qualifications, we have never been on the dole, yet still the banks refused us. The Yellow Pages offered us a "knifemaker" listing for the first time this year, after all these years of trying to get into it!'

Simeon enjoys the solitude of his lifestyle now and says he feels fortunate to be living in Australia. 'Peace and quiet are very important, but so is having plenty of things to do, as long as you occupy yourself with something you like doing. It would be sad if you had to make ten kilograms of cheese every day and you didn't like making cheese!'

NATIONAL PARK RANGER
Uluru, Northern Territory
Born: Darwin, Northern Territory, 1976

Dwarfed by the rich red rock above her, Teresa Atie is sharing a legend with the large group of tourists doing a base walk of Uluru (Ayers Rock). 'This walk is about the story of Mala, the hare-wallaby people,' she begins. 'Everything on this northern face of Uluru is connected to the Mala.'

Her simple delivery and fresh sense of humour make her easy to listen to, and the tourists are absorbed in her stories. This group has chosen to walk around the base rather than climb the rock at the request of the traditional Aboriginal owners, the Anangu People, who believe that the path of the climb is of great spiritual significance. The climb follows the traditional route taken by the ancestral Mala men.

'From what I've observed and been told, I feel it's sad that people still climb, disrespecting the wishes of the traditional owners. You see a lot of silly things — people going to the edge, for example, so you tell them not to chase after their hats if they blow away, and so on.

'Sometimes you're walking round the bottom and the climb is closed and the one question people will ask is: "When is the climb going to be open?" That's all they want to know. It makes you feel angry. I shouldn't show my anger towards them, but they have to know how we feel sometimes. I don't think it hurts, showing a bit of anger though, rather than always being pleasant like a ranger is supposed to be.'

Teresa has been a ranger at Uluru since January 1998.

The job fulfilled a long-held desire. 'I always wanted to be a ranger. The ones up north have a chocolate brown uniform and every time I see the uniform, it makes me tick,' she giggles.

'It's a privilege to be able to take care of something special. Just being here and feeling you're a part of it makes you feel like you're a special person, because it's famous and everyone knows it, and that makes it exciting. From the Aboriginal point of view, it's important to look after our sacred sites and make sure people don't harm them, and teach them how to respect our land.'

One of eight children, Teresa grew up on a reserve near Litchfield in the Northern Territory. Her Aunty Pam had the dominant role in her upbringing, teaching her bush skills and about her cultural heritage. 'I really loved her. We used to go out to the creek and do a lot of hunting and fishing. We caught turtles and dug for yams and she taught me how to make dilly bags and weave. I didn't care much about my brothers and sisters, because I looked up to my aunty and she treated me as her favourite. I suppose I was spoilt,' she admits.

At twelve years of age, Teresa was sent to boarding school in Lilydale, Victoria, a school 'full of different nationalities'. She had some trouble adjusting to the change of environment. 'I was a bit lazy and a bit naughty. The first time I was there, this boy said a really horrible thing to me, so I got my pencil case and whacked him with it.'

Teresa returned to Darwin to complete her two senior years of high school, then moved to Canberra, where she studied for her Parks and Wildlife Certificate. She was very surprised, she says, when she first got the job at Uluru. 'I had never visited it in my life before. When I first got to Alice, I asked how far it was to the rock and someone told me it was a six-hour drive. And here I was, wondering if I should take a taxi!' she laughs. 'I first saw the rock in the dark, and could only see the outline. The next morning it hit me. I looked out and there it was — this big giant red thing. At certain places when I walk round it, my hair stands on end and I think they're places I shouldn't be going.

'My mum told me that if there was a beautiful sunset on the first night here, then I was meant to be here. Well, there's lots of beautiful sunsets here but it was a nice one, and I got all goose-bumpy and emotional. There was this beautiful light with all these glowing colours. Sometimes there's horrible sunsets!'

Teresa has a range of duties, including maintenance and patrols of both Uluru and Kata Tjuta (the Olgas) parks, and conducting educational tours of the rock. Although she is not of the Anangu People, she is still concerned about preserving the culture of Uluru and conveying its significance to non-Aboriginal people.

'When I do the tours, I test myself and ask the people if they're understanding me. Sometimes you have to show a bit of emotion so you can get through to them. People turn off. They look too much at the beauty side rather than the meaning of the place. They look at the surface. Everything is connected — the rock, the sand, the leaves, the trees around it — if you put them all together, it's one big whole thing.

'I think it's important to get people to understand how life was for the Aboriginals living off the land and how hard it was back then — having to walk over the spinifex and find food. Even though it's modern times now, I think people are too focused on modern things. People are too dependent on shop tucker. I like to try and get them out of that wonderland.

'I've seen a lot of people doing the wrong thing and showing disrespect by taking photos of sacred sites, littering and damaging the place. It belongs to someone, it's someone's land. When you go to visit someone, you don't throw rubbish on their floor.'

Since living at Uluru, she is grateful for the knowledge she has received. 'I've learned about the sacredness of the rock. To me before, it was nothing. I've gone out with the old ladies and learned how to survive off the land. It's so amazing, how they find tucker here. I wouldn't have known this stuff before. You'd think blackfellas would know blackfella things,' she grins.

WUSHU AND TAI CHI MASTER

Brisbane, Queensland

Born: Guangdong, China, 1956

On a balmy Sunday morning in Brisbane's Chinatown Mall, Master Chen You-Nan is gently guiding a group of students through a tai chi class. Undistracted by the passing train of onlookers, they concentrate on his instructions, their minds and bodies focused on each deliberate, yet graceful, movement. This class is one of two weekend classes You-Nan offers free of charge. On Saturday mornings, he usually gets 100 people to Henderson Park, in the suburb of Sunnybank. He has gradually built up this following since establishing the Southern Shaolin Wushu (Chinese Martial Arts) and Tai Chi Academy at Runcorn, on Brisbane's south side, in 1998.

One of four children, You-Nan was raised at his grand-uncle's martial arts school in Guangdong, where he began studying kung fu at the age of six. 'Martial arts has a long tradition in my family. My grandfather is 105 and he still does kung fu now,' he says.

At twenty-one, You-Nan began studying Chinese martial arts at the Guangzhou Institute of Sports. He was elected captain of the Chinese National Wushu Team that same year. In subsequent years, You-Nan won two gold medals at the national wushu championships, and a gold medal in light-weight boxing.

After graduating, You-Nan served as head of Martial Arts and Boxing at Kee Narm and Wah Lum Si Farn Universities, and Zhangshan Medical College. During this time, he choreographed and starred in fight scenes in a number of Chinese films. In 1986, he was given a Best Instructor Award, which acknowledged him as one of the best wushu artists in China.

Through the early 1980s, You-Nan studied traditional Chinese medicine and massage. He believed this knowledge and wushu would complement each other. He also had a desire to bring his culture to Australia, and in 1988 decided to emigrate. He chose Brisbane because he thought there would be more opportunities for wushu instruction there, compared with Melbourne or Sydney.

When You-Nan arrived he spent two weeks washing dishes in a restaurant, but he soon made contact with some of his former wushu students from China and began teaching again. In addition to teaching, he took English lessons as well as working a number of odd jobs.

Through one of these jobs he met his wife Margaret, who emigrated from Taiwan in 1989.

In 1998 You-Nan's Southern Shaolin Wushu and Tai Chi Academy opened for business at the Runcorn location. Although he established the Academy in name in 1989, at that time he didn't have the kind of location he needed for his work. The premises, from which You-Nan also operates his acupuncture, massage and sports injury clinic, are located on the site of an old timber yard.

There are a number of different forms of wushu. Kung fu is divided into northern and southern styles, with the northern style emphasising leg movements and speed, and the southern style, which You-Nan teaches, relying on upper body strength and explosive power. The Southern style originated from the South Shaolin Temple, where Buddhist monks practised it for self-defence and exercise.

The obvious physical benefit of both kung fu and tai chi is fitness, but You-Nan believes they contribute to one's total wellbeing in a number of ways. 'Kung fu is like medicine for your bones and muscles. It is good for self-defence, and it teaches people, especially children, to be disciplined in themselves. I've also seen it help children with asthma. Tai chi is good for your chi — your

energy — your circulation and relaxation. I know this old man who was very sick and since he has been doing tai chi, he is much better, and he looks younger.'

It gives You-Nan great satisfaction to see his clients relieved of a persistent injury or a physical problem through his natural treatments. 'Chinese medicine is thousands of years old and millions of people have used it. It must be good,' he smiles. 'The modern (Western) doctor is very quick to cure a problem. They say, "Have a Panadol, it'll fix it", but everything is connected, and you need to consider the whole body. Using acupressure gets the circulation going well, without having to use medicine.

'In Australia people haven't always believed that the Chinese way could work. Since we've had the clinic, I have been seeing people who failed with normal doctors, but they see me and they leave happy. I like

to help people from the heart, and it helps me make friends too.'

You-Nan works seven days a week but says his job is always a pleasure. His week is usually a mix of seeing patients for acupuncture and massage, teaching his instructors, teaching classes and organising any specific events. The Academy is often called upon to perform lion dances at festivals and special events in Brisbane. One of his students has won twenty Queensland titles in kung fu competition, and some of his students appeared in the Jackie Chan movie, *First Strike*, in 1996.

You-Nan has returned to China a number of times, but Australia is very much home for him now. Naturalised in 1998, he and Margaret have a three-year-old daughter Lilian, and are expecting a son.

GYMNAST
Maroochydore, Queensland
Born: Toowoomba, Queensland, 1986

Carmen Huxley

The Saturday afternoon practice session has just begun at the Maroochydore Gymnastics Club. Carmen Huxley, the club's most experienced gymnast, is warming up with a few routines on the mat. It's hard not to notice her taut belly ('a six pack', as most would call it), the power in her legs, the strength in her arms, and the apparent ease with which she flings her body around. Like so many gymnasts, her most noticeable feature is her youth — she is thirteen. Carmen's coach, Kylie Shadbolt, a 1992 Olympian, is looking on, preparing to give the group of young girls a four-hour work-out.

Carmen was six when she first went to a gymnastics class. Her mother, Helen, says her daughter was more at home as a tomboy than in a tutu. 'Everyday things, like doing handstands or jumping on the trampoline or swinging made me want to get into it. I just wanted to go along and see how it was,' Carmen explains.

In the space of two years, Carmen began to move through the gymnastic levels very quickly. By the time her family moved from Toowoomba to Coolum, on the Sunshine Coast, she was beginning to take the sport fairly seriously. There are ten gymnastic levels, and she is currently at level eight. In October 1999 she competed at the national titles in Adelaide and was national champion on the beam in her level.

Competition makes Carmen nervous, but despite going red in the face and getting a churning stomach,

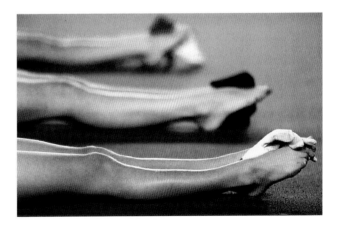

it heaps,' Carmen says, in her soft voice. 'I just didn't want to go. I love the coast too much.'

Carmen trains five evenings a week, from 5.15 to 8.30 pm, and on Saturday afternoons. After school she has a big afternoon tea and does her homework, then goes to training. She has dinner when she gets home, and goes to bed at 9.30 pm. On Sundays, she 'veges out', often going to the beach with the family. Her mother Helen says she doesn't push Carmen at all about gymnastics. 'It's entirely her decision whether she continues with it or not.'

Despite her commitment to training and obvious talent, Carmen is not aspiring to Olympic competition. She wants to reach level ten and travel to the USA to compete there, more for the experience than the glory.

Most of Carmen's good friends are from the gym rather than school. Her classmates don't really have an appreciation of the effort she puts in, or her achievements. 'They just say, "Yeah, that's great." They don't know what it is that I do really,' Carmen smiles.

Carmen is the highest level gymnast training at the club, and has found a role model in her coach. 'I used to look up to the bigger girls, but now they've all quit! I look up to Kylie, because if she doesn't explain something right, she does it for us, so we know what it looks like.'

A persistent heel injury, known as Sever's Disease, has been Carmen's only physical complaint in seven years of the sport, but she should outgrow it soon. 'The muscles get so tight that they don't allow the legs to stretch,' she says. 'I felt like giving up with it sometimes, but some acupuncture and physiotherapy has helped.'

Gymnastics consumes her life at the moment. She has little time for anything else, but she does enjoy doing art and craft. 'I'd like to be an artist or perhaps a gymnastics coach when I grow up, but I'm not really sure yet. I'm going to wait until I'm in high school to see what subjects I'm going to do.'

she still manages to stay focused. 'You just think of your technique and you do it. If you do your best at training, then you'll do your best in the competition. I set my goals, and my coach helped me get them.'

While participating at a clinic in Canberra in 1998, she was selected for a place at the Australian Institute of Sport, but after some careful thought and discussion with her parents, she decided against it. A decision to go would have meant relocation for the whole family. 'I was scared when I was asked, and I thought about

CATTLE STATION OWNERS

Mentone Station, Queensland

Born: Charters Towers, Queensland, 1923 & Brisbane, Queensland, 1946

SANDY

'Good morning Mentone. Are you there, Sandy?' a crackly voice comes over the UHF radio in the kitchen of Mentone Station. Sandy Whitehead gets up from his breakfast and grabs the mouthpiece to respond. 'G'day Alec, how are you?' he says to his nearest neighbour, who lives fourteen kilometres away. 'Are you heading into town today? Let me know if you are, I may need a few things.'

Mentone is a 33,000-acre cattle station, situated 125 kilometres north-east of Winton — what Sandy refers to as 'town' — and 130 kilometres south of Hughenden. From the tiny outpost of Corfield itself — population six — it is a thirty-minute drive along dirt road to reach the homestead. When it rains and the dirt becomes mud, there is no getting in or out of the property for days, sometimes weeks.

Sandy has lived on the station his entire life, apart from his years at boarding school in Charters Towers. His father drew the land by ballot in 1915 when it was sectioned off from Manuka, a larger property, and ran sheep on it. Sandy took over running the station in 1950, when it had about 13,000 sheep and four full-time employees. At shearing time, there would be up to eighteen men staying on the property.

Little has changed about the nature of the country here, according to Sandy, but advances in technology and communications have made outback living vastly

different. 'The heat and dust are the same as now. The rainfall averages haven't changed, nor have the summer temperatures,' he says matter-of-factly. 'I think electricity coming through made a difference. It meant we could put in cooking gear, fridges, a deep freeze and have power tools. You couldn't kill a bullock in the summertime once. You'd have fresh meat for a day, then you'd have to eat the rest as corned meat.

'The big thing that's made a difference is transport. In the sixties, there were some bad droughts and you couldn't shift your sheep anywhere, so you'd just try and save the nucleus of the breeding flock. Now you could have 20,000 sheep here and have the whole lot in New South Wales tomorrow if you wanted to.'

In the early 1970s, Sandy began buying a few cattle and reducing the number of sheep. By the early 1980s,

the price of wool was plummeting, so he gradually began switching to cattle. Since 1990, he has had only beef cattle. 'I think this country is more suited to sheep than cattle but obviously you can't have them if they're not a financial proposition.'

Sandy breeds Santa Gertrudis cattle and has Brahmans on agistment. He buys in 100 steers every year to maintain his population of around 1200. He sends a large truckload to market usually once a year. 'I just call Elders or Dalgetys and they'll offer me so much a kilogram. We take them to Winton and they go over the scales there. This year we got $1.18 per kilo for the Santa Gertrudis bullocks and $1.10 for the Brahman bullocks.'

An experienced horseman, Sandy did all the stock work on horseback during his first twenty-five years of managing the station. He also has a big interest in

country racing and is the secretary of the Corfield Race Club, which has been a race venue for 100 years. He has been a committee member of the Townsville Amateur Race Club since 1965. In the 1950s, 1960s and 1970s, Sandy bred and successfully raced a number of horses, with assistance from one of his ringers, who was a horse trainer. He is concerned about the demise of the country race meet. 'With the privatisation of the TAB, it could be bad for country clubs, because they'll only look at the shareholders. The city clubs is where people bet on the TAB and they'll be the ones looked after,' he says.

Sash and Sandy's son John returned to live at Mentone early in 2000, after eleven years working in Mt Isa. John will gradually take over management of the station, but Sandy will remain on the property. 'I hate the city, I hate Townsville now, with people running all over the place. I think it's free and easier in the bush. It just depends on what you're used to, I guess. I never think about what life would be like if I wasn't here.'

SASH

Sash knew nothing of the bush until 1963 when she left Brisbane to work at Upshot, a sheep station outside Longreach, as a governess to two young children. Despite its unfamiliarity, she fell in love with the outback immediately. 'I knew as soon as I got off the plane in Longreach that this was the place for me,' she smiles. 'I knew it was where I belonged. It just came so naturally to me. Nothing was a hassle.'

In 1965, eighteen months after her first posting, Sash moved to Daintree sheep station, fifty-four kilometres out of Winton, to teach three girls. The station owner, Ken Campbell-Brown, was a friend of Sandy's, and the mates would often visit each other, flying their Cessnas to each other's properties. Sandy soon befriended Sash and the two couples would go to the races or clay pigeon shooting together.

'Sandy would fly over to pick me up in his plane and I would get flying lessons on the way back to

but you still had to cook,' Sash sighs. 'I always had two or three extra people to cook for. In those days, we ate three big meals a day and had two smokos. I shudder to think if I had to do it now.'

The heat was something Sash put up with, but the flies were unbearable in the early days, a problem that has since been eliminated by the introduction of the dung beetle. 'Jackie was too lazy to shoo them off her face and she would have bung eyes from fly bites. The kids always wore fly veils under their hats when they went outside. Now days, there are hardly any flies.'

Sash home-schooled her children by correspondence and the School of the Air in their younger years, but sent them to boarding school for high school. She believes a bush upbringing makes for nice kids. 'The kids who come off the properties know how to work. They have a different outlook on life. They work from the time they're capable of working. They can drive a car as soon as they can reach the pedals, they can ride a horse, a motorbike. I think bringing them up out here was fantastic. They weren't subject to the bad things in life.'

Outback station living has become more expensive and few people can afford staff these days, which means a greater workload for the owners, according to Sash. There is more paperwork involved now, yet no time to read it, and then the jobs that have to be done, we struggle to get them all done on our own.'

Sash spends much of her time on photography these days, and has a darkroom in a 'donger' (a portable shed) behind the house. Since taking it up in 1990, she has turned it into a business, shooting country races, social events and anything else that happens in Corfield. The money she makes goes straight back into photographic equipment, but she loves it all the same and says she never runs out of things to photograph.

Sash's life is fuller, busier and far more social living at Mentone than it could ever be living in a city. 'I couldn't imagine life anywhere else. After two weeks in Brisbane I can't wait to get home. You want your space, you just get so used to space.'

Mentone. We would go out into the paddocks to check the cattle and sheep, and the fences and dams,' Sash recalls. It was a prelude of her life to come.

The relationship developed quickly, and Sash and Sandy were married on the Gold Coast in December 1965. After a three-day honeymoon in Sydney, Sash returned to Mentone and found herself immediately immersed in all the duties required of a station owner's wife, the constant one being cooking for the station hands. 'I certainly learned to cook in a hurry. I had a big old coke stove, an Aga. It was a beauty but in summer you had to keep your shoes on, as the floor got too hot. I was lucky to have a coldroom with its own engine. We ran a 240 plant Armstrong Sidley to generate our own power. There were no fans at night, because as soon as the engine was shut down for the night, that was it.'

All Sash and Sandy's children were born in a drought: Robyn in 1967, Jacqueline in 1969, and John in 1971. 'You went to hospital and came home with the baby,

THURSDAY ISLANDER
Rocky Point, Queensland
Born: Thursday Island, Torres Strait, 1929

The sea always seems to shimmer as Gladdy Pitt looks out towards Snapper Island from her home, perched on the cliff at Rocky Point, near Mossman. Most days, it still reminds her of Thursday Island, the homeland she was forced to flee at the age of eleven during the Second World War.

As Gladdy was getting dressed for school, a military sergeant arrived to tell her and her elder sister they should pack one suitcase each and prepare to board the troop ship, the SS *Ormiston*, which would depart at noon. 'You can imagine, all the belongings we had to leave behind. On the spur of the moment, we could take only the clothes we had on and another change. I was living with my sister — she had two little babies and I was helping her out — and she had to take nappies and clothes for them, so she couldn't fit much else in.'

The ship transported hundreds of women, children and elderly men to Cairns, leaving the fit young men — including Gladdy's father — behind on the island. Gladdy and her family moved in with her grandmother in Mossman, a town one hour north of Cairns. 'If you had relatives living here, then they had to put up with you, otherwise they shipped you off down south. Some of the elderly people taken down there died from the cold,' she says.

Gladdy remembers being excited about the array of fruits available when she first arrived in Cairns, but

feeling deep sadness about her predicament. 'To live in the place and know the war was on, when you had to do without such a lot of things, it was heartbreaking. Wherever you found a place to put your head, that's where you slept. Old Grandma put up with us. You just had to make room.'

Gladdy learned to read and write at a Catholic school on the island, but she never returned to school once she came to the mainland. 'They couldn't care less if we went to school or not. My sister did a lot of reading, so I read books with her. To have more schooling would have only been for a better job, but I was never in need of a better job. I had plenty of jobs. Look at these teenagers today, they get the dole. I didn't even know what the dole looked like!' she says emphatically.

At thirteen she got her first job as a house cleaner for the manager of the gas works in Cairns. She returned to Mossman at age fourteen to work at the first fish and chips shop in the town. In subsequent years she was a housekeeper at the Mossman and Post Office Hotels.

'Mossman was a real boom town,' she sighs. 'Things were much better then. There were plenty of jobs, you had the dance hall on Saturday night, the cinema … it was a social town. What have you got today? Nothing, because of television. People stay home and watch TV.'

Gladdy was eighteen when she met George Pitt, a local cane-cutter. 'I was young, and he would often come visiting. I went away working with a carnival for six months, thinking he might forget me, but who was there to greet me when I got back? So I ended up marrying him,' Gladdy smiles. At nineteen she had her first child, a boy. After having two more sons, the doctor advised her not to have any more children, but the couple's desire for a daughter was so great that they had another three children — and they ended up with six sons!

Living with her older sister had given Gladdy a good grounding in parenting skills. 'The boys weren't too bad, for some reason. I think discipline was stronger in those days. They were brought up in the tough times, when you made do with what you had. George never disciplined the children though — everything was left to me. I had to be the mean one!' she laughs.

George was a talented cane-cutter and earned a good wage. The couple spent the first two years of their marriage living in barracks on a cane farm, while George worked around different farms in the district. He would work from 7 am to 11 am, then from 1 pm to 5 pm, cycling home for lunch and a shower in the rest period.

The couple bought the block of land at Rocky Point in the 1970s and built the home Gladdy still lives in. They owned a small boat and would often go fishing in the waters directly opposite their home. When cane-cutters were replaced by mechnical harvesters, George went into fishing full-time, selling his catch to the Cairns Fish Board.

'When we first started fishing here, this reef opposite used to have all this long grass and you would hear all the fish in among the reeds. It was unbelievable. You could catch everything you needed just in this area. Now you go out there and you get nothing. These cane farms are so close to the edge of the bank that the soil run-off goes into the water and kills off the fish.'

Gladdy and George fished almost every day after George retired at sixty-five, taking their 'tinnie' into the Mossman or Daintree rivers and 'catching just about anything that swam'. They spent most of their time together after his retirement, fishing, shopping, seeing their children and grandchildren, and having a nap each afternoon.

On 17 September 1999, Gladdy woke from her nap and couldn't find George. 'I thought he'd be around the place somewhere, I thought he'd be home at three o'clock for smoko. I waited and waited, I had my smoko, and thought for sure he would turn up, but he didn't. The only place I hadn't looked was the back shed so I went and looked, and there he was, lying behind the door, stiff as a board. I shook him and shook him and called him, but he was cold. It made no difference. I rang up my son Ted, then I rang the ambulance. Ted gave him mouth to mouth, but he had already gone.'

George died from a massive heart attack; he was seventy-two. Gladdy had a stroke some weeks after his death, and now needs one of her sons to stay with her each night to keep an eye on her. 'I just got to cope, ay? As they say, life goes on,' she sighs.

Gladdy has never been back to Thursday Island, but longs to see it again. Although she left the island as a child, she believes she has retained its culture. 'I'm still an Islander. I can't see what's been lost in me. I'd like to go back there and have a look. One of my aunts told me the place is ruined, but I have to go and see for myself.'

WATER POLICE OFFICER
Gold Coast, Queensland

Born: Casino, New South Wales, 1955

The police boat, the *DW Wrembeck*, is out patrolling a stretch of the Broadwater, one of the busier Gold Coast waterways. The tourist capital of Queensland is built around water: its beaches, estuaries, rivers and man-made canal system mean there are thousands of kilometres of water to monitor. It's a weekday, so things are fairly quiet, but a few jobs will inevitably pop up in the course of the morning. There'll be some routine checks on the seaworthiness of some vessels, a few breath tests, and safety and licensing checks. In the

John Rice at the helm, with workmates

course of a month, chances are there'll be a boat accident to attend to, a body recovery, a search for a missing boat and an arrest for a break and enter.

At the helm is Senior Sergeant John Rice, officer in charge of the Gold Coast Water Police. Based here since 1983, John is the second longest serving water police officer in Queensland. When he first arrived, there were four water police officers. Now, he proudly states, there are twelve staff in the 'busiest water police station in the state'.

John wanted to be a police officer for as long as he can remember. He served a two-year cadetship at the Queensland Police Academy in Brisbane and was assigned to his first duties at Southport Police Station on the Gold Coast, in December 1974. 'It was all pretty ordinary stuff. I was learning how to deal with traffic accidents, and break and enters. Here was this eighteen-year-old constable getting his first life experience, seeing adult couples having domestics,' he recalls.

While John felt no different within himself when he became an officer, he felt other people's perceptions changed. 'I found I was looked at differently by members of the community once they found out who you were. It made a difference to the way you were accepted at a party, for instance, but you got to know how to handle it after a while.'

After a year at Southport, John was transferred to Sarina, near Mackay, for twelve months. In 1977 he went to Brisbane, where he worked on mobile patrols. That same year he married Trish, a police officer he had dated since his second year at the Academy. He spent eight years working as a detective in various stations around Brisbane before arriving at the Water Police in 1983. Having always had a love of boats and the sea, he never takes for granted the often coveted position he is in now. 'I think other police are jealous of us, in that they think we do for work what they do on weekends! But they don't appreciate that it is a specialist position, requiring specialist skills.'

Covering an area from Coolangatta, on the New South Wales–Queensland border, north to Moreton Bay, just south of Brisbane, the Gold Coast Water Police handle any routine police work that occurs on the water as well as search and rescues and boating accidents. The station is equipped with three boats, all named after officers who lost their lives in the line of duty; two jet skis; and an inflatable dinghy. 'We have two ambulance officers working with us full-time. All our boats are class-one ambulance vehicles. We can handle anything from a splinter in the finger to a major trauma,' John explains.

John says the greatest change he has seen on the Gold Coast is the increase in the number of boats, which inevitably means more search and rescue jobs for his staff. 'It's gone from being a quiet recreational area to a major boating port. South-east Queensland has 70,000 privately registered pleasure boats. The increase is just phenomenal.'

Two incidents stick in John's memory as his worst experiences: the drowning of a two-and-a-half-year-old child who wandered from his backyard into a canal; and a helicopter crash on Stradbroke Island in which seven people died. All seven victims were known personally to the Water Police staff at the time.

Dealing closely with these kind of tragedies means finding your own coping mechanisms, but it also leads to team bonding. 'You always try to remain remote from it,' John says. 'Having a wife who's an ex-officer helps, because she can relate to the pressures. Working in a tight-knit organisation, where we must rely on each other, also helps. Emergency service people always discuss things afterwards. We also sit down and have a beer with each other if it's been something traumatic.'

John believes that much of the police camaraderie comes from sharing difficult and stressful experiences. 'The police culture is something a lot of people treasure because it's like a big family. It's a hard job to do, and you know you'll get sustenance from the other officers.'

John intends to stay with the Water Police for as long as possible. 'It's such a rewarding job, and once you get the salt water in your veins, you want to stay.'

THRIFT SHOP MANAGER

Karumba, Queensland

Born: Aberdeen, Scotland, 1916

'G'day Grandma,' the middle-aged woman greets the white-haired old lady perched on her chair in a corner of the thrift shop. The woman picks up a couple of worn paperbacks and hands them over. 'That'll be one dollar please,' Bessie Joyce says sweetly to her customer. A young girl enters, wearing a dress she purchased earlier in the day. 'Hi Grandma,' she says.

'Show me the dress dearie,' Bessie beckons the girl over. 'I think it looks lovely on you.'

Bessie Joyce is 'Grandma' to everyone in Karumba, a remote coastal town on the Gulf of Carpentaria. Many people don't even know her first name, and Bessie can't quite remember how she got the title, but it doesn't matter. She's perfectly happy for everyone to call her Grandma.

When Bessie's 54-year-old husband died suddenly in 1970, she divided her possessions between her four daughters, packed her Valiant station wagon and left her home in Mullumbimby, New South Wales. 'I had too many happy memories and everywhere I looked in the home, I could see things that reminded me of him, so I thought: "I've got to get out of here before I go insane." So I got in my car and drove.' Bessie reached Mt Isa, and having always been fond of fishing, asked a local there about good fishing spots. He suggested Karumba. 'It took me two days to get here because it was just after the wet, and the roads weren't sealed. The first night I got bogged and had to be dragged out

by a fellow in a tractor, but I managed to get through the next day.

'The atmosphere of Karumba was good. It was a very friendly place and it was very much a hick, outback spot. I loved it. The first day I was here, I went out fishing and caught the biggest barramundi I've ever caught in my life. I didn't even know it was a barramundi, because I'd never caught one before!

'I dragged it up to the hotel on the edge of the river, and I said to the crowd: "What am I going to do with this fish? I can't eat it." And this fellow offered to take it. Well, that rotten skunk, he went straight to the pub and threw it on the counter and said: "Look what I've just caught!" He didn't even give me the honour of my catch. That was my initiation here,' she smiles, adding:

'Since then I've caught an awful lot of fish.'

Bessie has fished almost every day of the thirty years she has lived in Karumba, but she can't actually eat fish, so she always gives her catch away. 'I can put it in my mouth but it refuses to go down. Whether or not it's my guilty conscience of having caught the thing,' she giggles, 'I just don't know.'

Bessie's first home in Karumba was half a demountable building which she shared with the police station. She found a job with the Raptis fish company, then later in the kitchen at the pub. 'I found a lot of little jobs to keep myself occupied, and as long as it didn't interfere with my fishing, it was okay. There were only 100 people living here then. I loved the freedom of the isolation. I never had to lock the door; I felt safe here.'

someone to open up for me that day. I charge very little because it's all donated and we make a hundred per cent profit on everything. I'm quite sure there are a few people who survive on a shop like this, like some of the old men who live in the dongers [portable sheds] — they'll come in and buy something like a plate or a saucepan.' The biggest spenders in Bessie's little shop are the tourists, most of whom fill the town in the winter months and leave by the first week of September. In 1999, 100,000 tourists passed through here.

Bessie has experienced a number of floods in Karumba, and says the town usually gets cut off for two or three weeks during the wet season. 'The most dramatic thing that happened here was after the 1975 floods, when the water hadn't quite receded. I woke up one morning and looked outside, and there were millions — literally millions — of rats, back to back, all swimming everywhere. They got into everything. Even the dogs and cats got fed up with chasing them after a while. No-one knew where they came from, and they all just disappeared as quickly as they came.'

Bessie's house is next door to the boat ramp and overlooks the Norman River. She often spots crocodiles during her morning or evening fishing sessions and, at high tide, has seen them come very close to the ramp.

When she is not fishing, or working in the thrift shop, Bessie is cooking, usually for other people, or playing the poker machines at the Karumba Hotel. 'It's my one weakness, but I only allow myself $5 at a time,' she admits.

Three of her daughters live in Queensland and one in Darwin, and they come to visit her on a regular basis. Her 'real' grandchildren number six, and great grand-children three. 'My girls want me to visit them more, but I get bored. I'm not interested in shops and things.'

The winters are beautiful in Karumba, Bessie says, but the hot, wet summers always make her think about leaving for good. 'I hate the climate — the humidity makes you feel like a wet rag — and every summer, I say: "Just one more year." But I'm still here.'

Since 1991, Bessie has voluntarily managed Karumba's thrift shop, the only store in town where you can buy clothes, toys, linen and other essential items. To buy these kinds of goods new requires a long journey, either south to Mt Isa or east to Cairns, or a delivery by mail order. All the goods are donated, and once the $50 a week rental is paid on the premises, all the profit goes to the local childcare centre. Bessie opens the store three days a week but spends a lot of additional time sorting through bags of goods. She regularly sends excess bags of clothing to the remote Aboriginal missions at Mornington Island, Sweers Island and Bentinck Island.

'Only once have I ever had someone to help me when, for the first time in the history of Karumba, they took the pensioners out for an excursion, so I got

VETERINARIAN
Mackay, Queensland
Born: Brisbane, Queensland, 1975

The horse stands resolutely in the paddock as Dee-Ann Sheehy struggles to get a large steel contraption inside its mouth. Full of confidence, the young vet reaches deep inside the horse's mouth to file down his back teeth. 'You're doing fine matey,' she says soothingly to him, as the filing makes a spine-tingling sound. With that job completed, the next one is a pregnancy test on a mare. This also requires some competent horse handling, some patience, and a pair of long rubber gloves. The rest needs no description. It's by no means a glamorous task, but it's routine now for Dee-Ann, who has been working in Mackay since 1998.

Dee-Ann came to work for Stabler, Howlett and Lemmon, a large veterinary practice with five branches, a month after graduating from the University

of Queensland. She wanted to work as a mixed animal vet, and knew a regional position would give her this experience. 'As much as I love Brisbane, I didn't want to work there,' she says. 'I didn't want to work in a city. Brisbane is too big.'

Growing up, Dee-Ann lived in six different Queensland towns and attended five different schools. Her father was a stock inspector for the Department of Primary Industries, then worked for National Parks and Wildlife, so she was exposed to all kinds of animals from an early age. 'I liked all the moving around. We raised a lot of orphan native wildlife, like possums, wallabies, kangaroos, gliders and birds.'

It was by sheer fluke that Dee-Ann found herself studying veterinary science. 'When we lived at Lakefield National Park we had the flying doctor come regularly because there were always tourists putting fish hooks in themselves. So I thought I wanted to be a flying doctor. I had the grades, but I didn't get the uni entry level for medicine, so I put down vet science and somehow I got accepted. Once I was there, I didn't look back. I enjoyed it too much. The people in the course and the lecturers really made it. The vet students were down to earth and it didn't matter where you came from, they'd always be willing to help you. The vets usually have a rural background and they're there because they want to be there. They're not there because mum and dad think they should be.'

Dee-Ann lived in a Catholic women's college on campus for the first four years and spent most of her time with her head in the books, restricting herself to weekend socialising. She worked part-time in the college kitchen, and tutored younger students in her final two years.

Most of her holidays were consumed by practical work experience at vet surgeries.

After five years of study, Dee-Ann's university fees totalled approximately $13,000. Her parents have helped her to some extent, but she is still paying back the debt, which now comes directly out of her wages. 'When you first come out of uni, you get paid minimal wages for the first few years, you have a bomby car and there's a lot of financial pressure on you. Fees make education harder to get. I think it's too much to do full-time study and try and hold down a job.'

Dee-Ann admits she was nervous the first few weeks in her job, but says she was always assisted with any difficult procedures. 'My first consult by myself was an inter-digital cyst on a Doberman. He'd had it for years and years and the people were very frustrated by it. They'd never told us about inter-digital cysts at uni, and I'd never even heard of one!' she laughs.

'I panicked a bit and went out the back and had a quick read. These people had copped this young graduate who didn't have a clue what to do! So I talked to the senior guys about it and figured it out. At uni you're told to do what's best, but in the real world it's unfortunately what the owner can afford.'

Her first sudden death, a Labrador with gastroenteritis, came after eight months of work. 'I touched it and it died straightaway, so it was a shock, and I got upset. The difference between life and death is like that,' she says, snapping her fingers. 'You can't cry every time an animal dies. Most of the deaths are euthanasia requests. No matter what you're feeling, you can't take it with you to the next client. The most horrible thing is when you lose an animal, or put a pet down, and the next patient is a new puppy and you have to be excited for the client.'

Dee-Ann jokes that if she had a pet, it would be the most neglected animal in the neighbourhood because she is always at work. Her roster involves night and weekend work, as well as travelling up to 300 kilometres a week, but she also puts in some long hours of her own accord. She lives almost on the beach at Bucasia, but rarely finds time for a walk or a swim. 'I get up, have breakfast, and I'm at work all day. I come home at 8 or 9 at night, have dinner, and go to sleep.'

Although ambitious and passionate about her work, Dee-Ann says her career isn't quite living up to her expectations — yet. 'From a uni perspective, it's vastly different to what I thought it would be, but I'm doing more large animal work now. My favourite animal is probably the horse, but I enjoy dealing with cattle. It's a privilege working with any animal, really. What I plan to do is head overseas and get the UK perspective, which I have to do before I'm twenty-seven because of the work visa situation. Then I'll come back and settle down.'

The plethora of real-life television programs about veterinary work makes Dee-Ann cringe. 'Fair dinkum, I just can't watch those vet shows on TV. To do what I do, then come home and watch it as entertainment? Forget about it!' she laughs.

SUGAR CANE TRAIN DRIVER

Babinda, Queensland

Born: Babinda, Queensland, 1952

A thick swirling spiral of smoke climbs into the air from the Babinda sugar mill, dissolving into the steamy mist hanging over the green mountain ranges behind it. One of several sugar mills that dot this stretch of highway through north Queensland, this one looks much like the others — the white silos rising from the fields of green sugar cane, the little yellow trains packed full of freshly cut cane moving slowly along the tracks. At the wheel of one of these trains is Sam Terranova. He is a second-generation Australian whose father and two uncles bought a cane farm when they came to Babinda in 1924. They leased out the farm and ran a general store and drapery in town,

so Sam's experience with sugar cane didn't begin until he applied for a job at the Babinda mill when he was seventeen.

'I worked in a supermarket for ten months, but the wages were bad,' Sam recalls. 'Then I started working as a labourer at the mill. The wages were better, with shift allowances. I was working as a carrier on the wholestick trucks. They used to cut the cane in full lengths by hand then. The men would cut a row then go back and load it on to the truck. Cutting by hand stopped around 1976. Now, it gets cut into pieces by harvester and automatically put into bins.'

Four seasons on, he began driving the locomotives. 'I didn't mind the locos. Mechanically it was something I picked up easily because I like machinery,' he says.

Sam is one of about thirty locomotive drivers working at the Babinda mill. They cover three shifts in a twenty-four hour period and travel within a twenty kilometre radius of the mill, collecting bins of cut cane from the surrounding farms. Sam usually drives a double-headed locomotive, which can carry up to 130 bins. It takes twelve months for a cane plant to reach maturity. The crushing season, between June and December, lasts between twenty and twenty-six weeks. Once the cane is crushed and processed, it is transported to a sugar refinery in Brisbane.

In thirty years of driving the trains, Sam has only had one accident. 'I ploughed into a tractor sitting on the line. I don't know what his game was, I was on the horn, hitting him with my lights, and he would have seen me coming. He tried to reverse, but it was too late.'

Sam and his brother inherited 125 acres of land from their father. They continue to grow cane on it, but severe floods in 1998 and early in 2000 wiped out most of the crop. 'This area is particularly prone to flooding so we don't stand to make anything out of our cane for a while now,' Sam explains. 'When I'm out driving the locos I think I'd rather be farming, but I've got no choice — the locos are my livelihood.' Sam is not optimistic about the mill in his town, and is disappointed Babinda is not the thriving community it was in the 1970s. 'I can't see much future in the mill here. Maybe I'm pessimistic, but I think eventually part of the crop from this area will go to the Gordonvale mill, and elsewhere. They'll just end up transporting the cane further distances.

'The town has changed a hell of a lot since the cane-cutter days. It's gone backwards and it's just about a ghost town now. It's deteriorated. I like where I live, but I think the town could improve more. We need to do something about fixing it up. I suggested to the real estate agent we start promoting it again. You never get better-running creeks than you do here, we have mountain streams running all the time and beautiful clean water.'

During the off season, Sam does maintenance work in the mill, but he also spends a couple of months away each year, tin mining at Mt Garnet, 150 kilometres inland from Babinda. 'I'm in partnership with my brothers. We have our own mining leases. I just have to have a break away from the sugar industry,' he explains.

The shift work has taken its toll on Sam, and he soon plans to restrict himself to daytime hours. He has diabetes, which is exacerbated by an erratic diet and sleeping habits. 'I'm not a real sugar supporter!' he laughs. 'Both my parents had diabetes, so I knew I was getting it. It gets worse after night shift.'

Sam lives with his 75-year-old mother, in the same house he grew up in. He has never married. 'I guess I just left my run too late,' he says uneasily.

His home, which was once the grocery store his father ran, is on the old Bruce Highway and looks out towards the mill and the mountains behind it. It's very picturesque, but Sam doesn't pay much attention to the scenery. 'I guess we don't appreciate the area enough, because we've been here so long,' he says.

CONTRACT HARVESTER

Roma, Queensland

Born: Birchip, Victoria, 1962

It's raining in Roma, and Trevor Botharas and his team of workmen are waiting out the weather in the Roma Caravan Park. For two days the rain has delayed their wheat harvest, putting them behind schedule. While they wait, they attend to a few odd jobs, like servicing the truck, but there isn't much else to do today but sit around and wait. As soon as the sun comes out long enough to dry out the grain, they'll be harvesting, then moving on to the next town.

Roma is one of eleven stops on a four-and-a-half-month journey through Queensland, New South Wales and Victoria to the South Australian border. Trevor established his contract-harvesting business in 1988 with one machine, a burnt-out header he had purchased from an insurance company and then rebuilt.

Trevor first drove a harvester at the age of fourteen on his family's 2000-acre wheat and sheep property. He served a mechanic's apprenticeship with an International Case dealer and developed an interest in farm machinery. 'I'd always wanted to do harvesting and buying this header gave me a break into it. I believed there was a need for it in the area. I began with local work at first, then by word of mouth it grew,' he explains.

Contract harvesting is more customary among crop producers now. 'There has always been a certain amount of harvesting contracted, but now because of the quality of grain required, you have to get the harvest

done quickly without any weather damage, so it's more readily accepted. Also, because the price of machinery has risen so much, a lot of farmers can't justify having their own machinery. We got one new machine this year and it cost $290,000.'

Trevor now employs up to five people in peak season and has three machines, a tractor and a chaser bin. From his home town of Birchip in Victoria, he goes on the road at the end of September and heads to Roma in Queensland. After a month in Queensland, he heads south again, to New South Wales and Victoria. The stops on his tour are Roma, Surat, Condamine, Goondiwindi, Coonamble, Rankin Springs, Kyalite, Birchip, Horsham, Kaniva and Kilmore.

The first trip north is 1800 kilometres and very slow, because the machines only go forty kilometres an hour. This first leg takes fifty hours. It is expensive to transport the machines on trucks, so they are usually driven.

Accommodation for the harvesting team is in farm cottages or shearers' quarters, or the caravan they bring with them. The team all have farming backgrounds. This fact, along with the quality of the machinery, makes Trevor confident in business. 'It's a very competitive industry, but we won't cut our prices just to get a job. We believe our service and the reliability of our machines gives us an edge,' he says bluntly.

Trevor will not take his machinery any further north than Roma because of the parthinium weed. This weed, a threat to crops, is prevalent in northern Queensland, so it is a risk to put the machinery in these areas. 'Some of the properties won't use us if we have been into the parthinium weed areas,' Trevor explains.

The total crop harvested on Trevor's tour is usually

between 24,000 and 27,000 acres. He harvests all grains — wheat, barley, canola, beans, chick peas, peas and lentils and, sometimes, millet and sunflowers. His job is simply to harvest the grain and tip it into trucks organised by the farmer. Timing is crucial. 'There's always pressure on us time-wise. The farmers won't wait for harvesting. If the timing is wrong, it could decrease the price of the crop substantially. One bad storm, say, could drop the price by $50 a tonne.

'All we can do is make sure the sample is up to scratch and make sure we harvest at the right moisture level so the silos accept it into the system. With harvesting, there's no second chances. The farmer has spent twelve to fifteen months preparing it and if we muck up, that's the farmer's income for the year. We have to develop a good relationship with the farmer.'

The most significant change Trevor has seen is the advancements in machinery in the late 1990s. 'Everything is electronic now. It's not hard to keep up with, but it's expensive to keep the machinery up to date. The price farmers are getting for their produce is at its lowest point and they've been forced to become more efficient to remain profitable, and we've had to do the same. People are going for more alternative crops now, because the profit margin is higher. Canola, chick peas and lentils have taken a real surge lately.'

In the non-harvest season, Trevor services machinery in his local area and runs a share farm. His wife Jenny handles the accounts and bookwork through the year.

He has lived in Birchip his whole life and has no desire to live anywhere else. He would like to expand his farm and grow more crops. 'It's not a bad place. You know everyone who lives there. Life is what you make it in a small town.'

Although it takes him away from his wife and three young children, Trevor enjoys the harvesting sojourn each year. 'You learn something every day, you see so many different work practices. Every year is different, every crop is different,' he smiles.

MINER

Mt Isa, Queensland

Born: Mt Isa, Queensland, 1965

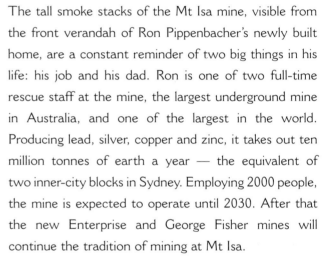

The tall smoke stacks of the Mt Isa mine, visible from the front verandah of Ron Pippenbacher's newly built home, are a constant reminder of two big things in his life: his job and his dad. Ron is one of two full-time rescue staff at the mine, the largest underground mine in Australia, and one of the largest in the world. Producing lead, silver, copper and zinc, it takes out ten million tonnes of earth a year — the equivalent of two inner-city blocks in Sydney. Employing 2000 people, the mine is expected to operate until 2030. After that the new Enterprise and George Fisher mines will continue the tradition of mining at Mt Isa.

Ron began working at the Mt Isa mine in 1981, following in the footsteps of his father Josef, who had given up the butcher's trade in 1966 to work in the mine. Two years after he began his diesel-fitting apprenticeship, Ron went underground for the first time, feeling very nervous in the 1000-kilometre plus maze of tunnels.

'It's like … an environment you can never imagine,' Ron struggles to explain. 'The trip down in the lift is difficult. You're in a cage with two decks, squashed in like sardines and there's ninety-two men on each deck. The first day, when we had to go to the ore body, if I had lost my mate, I wouldn't have found my way back.'

A tag board system in each area indicates the location of each miner. At the beginning of each and every shift, a miner is required to answer three questions on a 'safety sheet': What am I about to do?

What could go wrong? What do I do to stop it going wrong? This ensures the miner is alert to potential risks, and aware of safety procedures. As a safety incentive, Mt Isa Mines makes a donation to each miner's chosen charity, according to his length of time without accidents.

By 1986, Ron had decided to join the mine rescue team, initially as one of the volunteer regular miners who assist the team's full-time members during rescues. That same year, Ron's father Josef was killed in an accident. Mercifully, Ron wasn't at work that day. 'Dad worked at what you call nineteen level, just one kilometre underground. It was a haulage level. He was killed in a mud rush. He was on his own in this section of mine where they were using an explosive to bring the material down. They had a spillage, the ore rushed down and spilled out. It took a long time to find him. They didn't

know until he didn't report in at the end of his shift.'

Ron holds no bitterness about his father's death. While he is accepting of the fact that mining can be dangerous, he doesn't appreciate the public perception of it. 'The funny thing with the mining industry is that you always seem to go to court guilty. In normal civilian life, they have to prove you're guilty, but in mining you have to prove your innocence,' he sighs.

In 1989 Ron became a full-time rescue staffer, responsible for training and maintenance as well as rescues. There are usually nine major incidents a year and, of those, six will involve rescues. Fire is the greatest risk, but rock falls, flooding, cave-ins, explosions and machinery all pose a threat to human life.

'We get more than 100 underground fires a year, and three of those usually escalate,' says Ron. 'Each unit has a fire extinguisher so the hope is that most of the

"PREPARED FOR THE WORST - GIVING OUR BEST"

fires will be put out quickly. With a fire, we usually co-ordinate teams from the surface. There is nowhere for the smoke and heat to go, and fire can move up or down the ventilation shafts very rapidly. The smoke also means it can be difficult to locate people. You can't see your hand in front of your face sometimes. Water can also cause big problems. Once, we had some water which was flowing into a tunnel at forty-five litres a second and we had to pump it out a long way to get rid of it.'

In an emergency, a mine rescuer needs to carry an extraordinary amount of equipment. 'You've got your torch, radio gear, breathing apparatus, first-aid kit, lifting equipment, a stretcher, drinking water, and it all adds to your weight.' Because miners can dehydrate very quickly, chilled drinking water is always available underground. 'Some guys drink twelve litres of water in a twelve-hour shift. This is the secret to working in a mine, to stay hydrated,' Ron explains.

Training the volunteer team for potential accidents and general safety training for everyone consumes most of Ron's time. 'Our training is very tough here. I've burned my ears a few times while training in a fire tunnel. Hopefully, in real situations, it will always be easier.' His worst experience as a rescuer came in 1999, when a man was buried in a shaft by big rocks. 'It was very difficult because he wanted to come out one way and I had to convince him to come out another way. Any false move and it would kill him, so that was very tricky. I got too involved with it. He was okay but he's never worked underground again.'

In ten years in the rescue team, Ron has seen ten deaths. He says most people involved in a mine accident never work underground again, because of their stress levels. He believes his own personality is suited to the job. 'I don't mind a bit of stress but, you know, basically I'm a steady person and not too many things worry me.'

Ron and his family live at Breakaway Creek, a new development on the outskirts of the western Queensland town. Whenever his beeper goes off, which is quite often, it's only an eight kilometre trip back to the mine to co-ordinate a rescue. 'I like the remoteness here, two minutes out of town and you're in the bush. If you want to be quiet you can be quiet. There's plenty of wildlife around. It's a great place to bring up kids and the education system is quite good here. The amount of people who have left Mt Isa and come back is just incredible. As the old Mt Isa saying goes, once you've drunk the water from the Leichhardt River, you'll always come back.'

Ron feels there is a general misconception about the place of mining in the world and its effect on the environment. 'A lot of people don't realise that everything in today's modern world is mined. Things either come from the earth or they're grown. In televisions, there's lead to make them safe. Electricity comes from copper, the cars we drive come from steel, windows from sand mining.

'I think a lot more companies are environmentally conscious now. With our copper smelting, we're taking away the waste gas and turning it into sulphuric acid for use in fertiliser. We eat fruit and vegies but without the fertiliser and the farm equipment which comes from mining, we're going to struggle. I think with responsible mining there is a balance that can be achieved.'